CHRISTIANITY
and
COMMUNICATION

F. W. DILLISTONE

Dean of Liverpool

CHARLES SCRIBNER'S SONS

New York

CONTENTS

Preface

I HAVE tried in this book to approach the problem of communication from the Christian point of view. When the manuscript was nearly ready for the printer the comprehensive volume entitled *Studies in Communication* came into my hands. In his introduction Sir B. Ifor Evans tells how a Communication Research Centre came into being at University College, London, and how Professors from all departments willingly collaborated in a study of the problems involved. A striking omission from the impressive list of contributors is any representative of Theology, and although this is explainable on the ground that there is no Department of Theology at University College yet there is little doubt that whatever the value of its own contribution might have been, Christian Theology in particular would have stood to gain enormously by sharing in such a co-operative enterprise.

For Christians have from the beginning lived within the context of an overmastering constraint. " Ye shall be witnesses unto me both in Jerusalem and in all Judæa, and in Samaria, and unto the uttermost part of the earth." " We cannot but speak the things which we have seen and heard." It is true that there have been periods in the history of the Christian Church when some have lost all sense of this responsibility, and others have been prevented by outward circumstances from fulfilling it to any marked degree. But that Christianity, if it is to be true to its original character, must continue to be deeply concerned about the principles and techniques of effective communication is surely obvious. Through the experience of nearly 2,000 years it has much to contribute: in view of the rapid changes in modern methods of communication it has much to learn.

In chapters two and three I have gone back to first principles in the attempt to discover what are the unchanging factors in all processes of human communication. In chapters four and five I have made a rapid survey of the history of communication within an expanding Christendom. Finally, in the last four chapters I have applied the results of these earlier inquiries to the situation as it exists to-day. I recognise that certain large theological and historical questions are touched upon only lightly and even superficially, but I hope that at least in some small measure the book will make a contribution to what may be called the theology of communication.

Nothing would give me greater satisfaction than to know that this study of *principles* had been of some use to those who are urgently engaged in the *practice* of Christian communication. I think in particular of the Church Missionary Society within whose fellowship I once had the privilege of serving and whose courageous grappling with the problems of the modern world I so greatly admire. But everywhere to-day the situation is a missionary one and the Church's most difficult task is that of communicating the Gospel into the new technological age. To those whose position is in the front line, I offer the reflections of one who has tried to wrestle in mind with some of their problems in the comparative safety of the rear.

My thanks are due to the Rev. Colin Elliott, Vicar of St. Paul's, Southport, who was good enough to read the typescript and to make a number of most helpful suggestions.

CHAPTER ONE

Bridging the Gulf

I. THE PROBLEM OF COMMUNICATION

DURING THE past five years I have become increasingly aware of the importance which effective communication is assuming in every department of life. One week a letter to the press emphasises the difficulties of the educator seeking to impart information to a generation whose attitude of mind and mental processes are vastly different from his own. Another week a letter deplores what it calls the " breakdown in communications " in national life, a breakdown which is particularly evident in the field of industrial relations. A local branch office of a trade union cannot understand the language in which it is addressed from Headquarters : the factory worker cannot grasp the quite elementary economic truths which the management is anxious to convey to him. How can a common system of signals be established ? Where can a common language be found ?

Yet this situation has arisen in a world in which man's knowledge of the *techniques* of communication has increased by leaps and bounds. Distance no longer presents any major difficulty. The time-lag in transmitting information is largely a thing of the past. Even the human agent can span oceans in a matter of hours and can discharge his communication-responsibility face to face. As far as technical ways and means are concerned there seems to be no obstacle which cannot ultimately be overcome.

Nevertheless the problem remains. At Lake Success, for example, every modern device has been introduced to enable the delegates to hear what is being said, each in his own tongue. A speech made in Russian can be heard almost simultaneously in English or in French. But does this automatically lead to the communication of the speaker's real meaning to his hearers ? Unfortunately it does not. Cardinal Griffin was speaking only too truly when he declared that " the most disturbing feature of modern statecraft is that we have not the slightest idea what many leaders mean by the terms they use and, not to put too fine a point on it, very little reason for believing that they mean anything at all."

Even in the realm of business where unlimited resources are available for the employment of the finer arts of salesmanship and the latest advertising techniques there is a growing concern because of an apparent failure to establish a proper connection with the minds of potential buyers. When the magazine *Fortune* made a nation-wide survey of the situation it had little fault to find with the media of mass-communication. But it was still compelled to ask the question : " Why isn't Joe Doakes listening ? " Its main conclusion about possible remedies, " Only with trust can there be any real communication," is exceedingly suggestive but the question still remains as to how such trust is to be created, how the intangible quality which we call confidence can be strengthened and increased.

Wherever then we look—to the fields of politics, of economics, of education, of social relations—we find that men are concerned about the possibilities of better communication. Sometimes what is at stake may seem comparatively trivial, but more often a society's very existence may be involved,[1] and even the survival of world civilisation. It is when we envisage two cultures standing over against one another—each with its own presuppositions, its own myths, its own social patterns and ultimate goals— that we begin to recognise the magnitude of the problem of communication and at the same time its critical importance. For two such cultures cannot remain for ever shut away in separate compartments. Either improving communication and deepening trust or the reverse. When communication ceases, hatred and destruction are never far away.

II. THE CULTURAL GULF

Let us look a little more carefully at the gap which may exist between cultures. Imagine, for example, the life and activity of a predominantly agricultural community. The land is guarded with jealous care and tended with patient devotion : men and women

[1] Cp. J. Z. Young. Doubt and Certainty in Science. p. 7.

gain their particular status by virtue of their relationship to the process of food production : the times and seasons gain their significance by reason of the place they occupy within the recurring cycle of nature. Methods of work, myths and symbols, codes of conduct, all belong to the particular cultural pattern which such a society represents and to which it makes its continuing contribution.

But over against this imagine a culture growing out of the life and activity of a mobile pastoral community. Certain bases of operation or places of encampment gain a temporary significance but there is no deep attachment to the earth : the character of the work to be performed involves little division of labour or gradation of functions : times and seasons gain their significance according to whether they are propitious or dangerous for travel and change. Again work, ethic and art are all expressions of the cultural pattern, though they in turn exercise a reciprocal influence upon the culture to which they belong.

Now one culture may be more fluid and flexible than another, and individual non-conformists can exercise a great influence. Nevertheless great cultural entities have existed in history, and the more settled and ingrown they have become the harder it has been for them to communicate with one another. Individuals and groups who have grown to maturity in one culture find that their whole approach to the method and meaning of existence is different from their contemporaries in another culture. To find common ground or connecting links seems an almost impossible task.

In our own day the cultural gulf finds its most conspicuous expression in the division between traditional societies whose structure depends upon agriculture and trade, and the rapidly expanding new society in which science and technology are the controlling cultural factors. I do not suggest that it is possible to make any hard and fast distinction, for within any single nation both cultural patterns are to be found and even where the influence of the scientific outlook is most pronounced, vestiges of the culture whose focal points are the land and the rhythm of nature still exist. At the same time the division is becoming more marked every day and the contrast between the organic outlook, belonging to man's life in dependence upon nature, and the technological outlook, belonging to man's consciousness of his control of natural forces, ever more pronounced.

The importance of this division for the continuing task of communication is not hard to discern. How can a man whose very existence is geared to the machine—to the necessity for regularity, efficiency, and immediacy of results—open his imagination to receive a communication emanating from a world where long patient processes and steady organic growth constitute the dominant pattern of development? How can a culture whose whole attention is focused upon the factual, the observable, the verifiable, the workable, suddenly turn aside to consider the unseen, the personal, the ethical, the eternal?

Such questions do not concern only the preacher and the educator. They are of vital importance to the politician, the social worker and to the leader of industry itself. But they cannot fail to press heavily upon those whose special task it is to communicate religious truth. How can the Christian Gospel, for example, a message originating from the pre-scientific world, be made comprehensible to the ordinary man of the modern technological age? This is the way Rudolf Bultmann (one of the most distinguished New Testament scholars of our time) has framed the essential question and his answer is still under vigorous debate. For Bultmann believes that it is possible to remove all mythological concepts and ideas from the essential New Testament message and to present it afresh to scientific man in a way that he can understand.

Bultmann's radical solution can best be described in his own words. " The language of the Bible," he writes, " is mythological. People pictured the universe then in terms of heaven above and hell beneath, of the heavenly Son of God descending to earth and again ascending to heaven, of the kingdom of heaven over against the domain of the prince of evil and so on. But to-day man thinks in terms of science, not of mythology. Modern man lives in a a world in which life makes constant use of technical means created by science. Mythological thinking is quite foreign to him. Therefore we must picture the universe and man's place in it in terms of the scientific thinking of our own day, allowing the Gospel, the truth of which is independent of any picture of the world, to meet our existence at the deepest level and to bring us to God through Christ."

In this forthright statement, Bultmann declares in effect that there is no possible way of throwing a bridge over the gulf that separates the mythological world from the scientific. But this need not trouble us unduly, he thinks. The Gospel strikes to the heart of man's existence wherever he is. There is therefore no need to communicate the Gospel from one age to another or from one culture to another. It is "independent of any picture of the world." So long as it negates man's existence-in-death and affirms man's existence-in-life its essential task has been performed.[1] But this can be done, Bultmann declares, without reference to man's world or to his cultural forms. *The* Death, *the* Resurrection are all-sufficient. Such a solution will not satisfy many. Yet there is little doubt that Bultmann has exposed a situation where the cleavage between cultures is as wide as it has ever been in human history. Modern scientific world-pictures are totally unlike any pictures belonging to the pre-scientific age, and to communicate truth which claims to be timeless in its relevance but which was originally expressed in terms drawn from that pre-scientific world seems an almost impossible task.

[1] Bultmann holds that man in his ordinary existence is actually the prisoner of his natural surroundings and is under constant threat of the death which must ultimately engulf him. Moreover, because of his sinful concern with self-assertion and self-justification, he is at every stage dead to the life of the spirit. Only as he is identified with the Christ in death and resurrection can his existence become at any moment an existence-in-life.

III.   THE TASK OF THE MISSIONARY

There are gulfs between groups of different ages, between societies occupying different levels of economic status, between different cultural traditions. In each case it is exceedingly difficult to establish effective communication. Finally, and perhaps most difficult of all, there is the task of the missionary, who, reared in a particular environment, belonging to a particular culture, speaking a particular language, committed to a particular religious faith (which may have only a loose connection with the culture to which he belongs) seeks to communicate that faith to those whose environment, culture, language and religion are altogether different from his own. His ultimate aim is to reach that place where he can speak face to face with his fellow-man in the other culture and speak in such a way that the deep of his own existence is communicating with the deep in the existence of the other. But how can he do this ? It is not just a matter of learning new words and forms of expression in another language. The aim can be nothing less than a fullness of communication from one side of the gulf to the other.

From the beginning Christian missionaries have been compelled to take account of at least four factors.

(1) *The essential message to be communicated.* Though at first sight it might appear that this factor would present little difficulty, it actually involves issues as

complex as any of the others. What is the essential
Christian message? Is it simply the proclamation of
who Jesus was and what He did? Even if this is the
essential message, can it be expressed adequately and
meaningfully apart from some surrounding context
of ideas and events? Can it, for example, be separated
completely from the Jewish context within which it
originally took shape? If not, how much of the context has to be retained? Further, can any additions
be brought in from other national or cultural contexts to enable the essential message to take on
meaning in a new environment?

Answers to these questions have ranged from the
severely simple, which urges that the only essential
message is that a divine being came into the world to
save sinners, to the highly complex, which requires
that the whole setting, either of the canonical
Scriptures or of Church tradition, be accepted as an
essential framework, apart from which the Christian
message cannot be received or understood. This is
not merely an issue which has prominence through
the missionary endeavours of modern times. It clearly
arose as early as the period covered by the New
Testament, for in its writings the basic question of
how a faith which was gendered and born in an almost
exclusively Jewish setting could be defined and
expressed and communicated within a setting which
was almost exclusively Greek is already being asked.
Can the essential message be stripped of its historical
antecedents and of its cultural determinants and then
sent forth naked and unashamed into whatever new

environment is open to receive it? I shall try to answer this question at a later stage.

(2) *The character of the messengers who are the communicators.* By "character" I do not mean moral qualities. That the messenger must be devoted and sincere, neither proud nor self-assertive, goes without saying. But there are subtler characteristics (related, it is true, to moral qualities) which are of great importance in one who seeks to communicate a particular message within an alien environment. How far should he try to divest himself of his own former manner of life? There are basic matters such as food, clothing, housing, work. There are also more intangible matters such as social customs and conventions, reading and conversation, travel and recreation. What policy is the communicator to pursue in relation to all of these things?

Again answers have ranged from the severely simple, which affirms that the communicator must leave all behind except his essential Christian integrity and his essential Christian message, to the highly complex, which urges that he must constantly be engaged in gathering up into his own person the wholeness of the Christian tradition, out of which he has come and to which he belongs, and relating it to the wholeness of the new cultural environment within which he now lives. These different answers have their implications not only for the character of the communicator but also for the character of what might be called the communicating "task force" to which he belongs.

If it be decided that the severely simple answer just outlined is not adequate, then it must necessarily follow that the communicator cannot indefinitely proceed and act alone. He must hold fast to certain social and organic relationships or he will be unable to carry forward the continuing task of confronting the wholeness of the new culture with the wholeness of the Christian tradition.

(3) *The character of the means and channels of communication available at any particular period of history.* Here factors are involved which play a most significant part in effective communication. It has often been pointed out that the communication of the Gospel in the early days of Christian missions was largely made possible by the existence of the remarkable roads which had been constructed by Roman engineers, by the comparative ease of sea travel in the Mediterranean basin, and by the system of law and order which had been established within the Roman Empire. Certainly the great expansion of missions since the sixteenth century has followed on the development first of the sailing ship and then of the steamer. Spanish, Dutch and British sailors have pioneered sea-routes and guarded ships from molestation and missionaries have often taken advantage of the facilities thereby offered to them. In more modern times travel by air has greatly assisted the advance of the ecumenical movement, a movement which is intimately related to the ongoing missionary enterprise. Thus the means of travel available to the communicator is at all times an important factor. It

has a real bearing upon the economy, the personnel and the strategy of missions.

But not only are the means of travel important. The available channels of communication have also to be taken into account. Here problems immediately arise. An effective channel of communication in one area may not be suitable in another. (Open-air preaching in bazaars such as has been common in India and China could not be effectively employed in Greenland or even in a noisy city.) A technique of rapid communication suitable in the West may be quite ineffective in parts of the East. Even more important, there is the question of whether a particular channel or technique of communication is really able to convey the essential Christian message. (Who can say whether a play can be effectively communicated through the channel of television?) What are the relative values of the sermon, the mystery play, the printed page, the film, the broadcast, the strip cartoon, for the communicating of the Gospel? Some of these questions will come up for consideration later, but for the moment enough has been said to show that means and channels and techniques need the most careful attention and evaluation at every period of Christian history.

(4) *The relationship between the respective languages of giver and receiver in the process of communication.* No gulf seems wider and deeper than that which separates two language areas. When there is a common language, whatever misunderstandings may arise through peculiar idioms or odd usages, there is always the

sense that a great common area of tradition and understanding already exists. But when there is no meeting-point in language, when the only available channels are signs and gestures, then effective communication seems to be out of the question. The essential preliminary to all other activities is to begin to relate my language system to the language system of the other so that gradually information from the one can be transposed effectively into the other.

But few tasks in the world are more difficult than the work of translation. A language is a living organism which has grown and developed through centuries of social history and is still in process of adapting itself to new situations. No element in the language can stand completely alone, and it is therefore impossible to take one element and find its exact equivalent in another language. Only the man who has really lived himself into another language until it has become second nature to him, is competent to take affirmations and statements from his own mother tongue and transpose them into the other language medium.

In the case of the Christian message, the problem is complicated still further by the fact that the communicator is dealing with an interpretation of reality which was originally conveyed to men through the common Greek of the first century and brought into the vernacular of the European peoples more than a millennium later. Now from these tongues the second great transposition has had to be made into the languages of Africa and the Orient, and it is hardly to be wondered at that the task has scarcely begun. Pioneer translations have indeed been made but new revisions and new translations must constantly be in process of production if the task of finding the adequate forms to convey the distinctive Christian message against the background of a particular world-view is to be effectively performed. As the means and techniques of conveying information through world channels become more and more efficient, the problems of language-relationship will become more and more acute. If the Christian Gospel is indeed a message for the whole world no single group can be more affected by and concerned with these problems than the ecumenical Christian Church.

CHAPTER TWO

The Image and the Word

I. BUILDING AND SHARING

TWO CHANNELS of communication are of universal significance in the life of mankind. First of all, man's sense of *sight* enables him to receive a wealth of visual images into his own inner consciousness and at the same time his imagination enables him to construct patterns of line, colour and gesture which convey images to the consciousness of his neighbour. Secondly, man's sense of *hearing* makes him aware of an extraordinary diversity of sounds in the world around and at the same time he is able to construct patterns of words and music which serve as means of communicating with his fellow-men. Seeing and Hearing, the Visual Shape and the Tonal Shape, the Image and the Word—these are the communication-pairs through which information is transmitted and received the world over. It is with these that I shall be constantly concerned for not only are they of supreme importance in all processes of human inter-communication but they are also, in the Christian view, of unique importance in the self-revelation and self-communication of God Himself to man.

If it be asked which of the two has the greater significance, no obvious and immediate answer can be given. It is generally agreed that things seen produce a more pervasive and permanent effect than is the case with things heard. On the other hand, the range and adaptability and challenging character of the sound-medium is probably far greater than that of sight. Again, whereas images seem to penetrate more deeply into the mysterious reaches of man's unconscious life, words are unrivalled as instruments of order and precision in man's conscious life. But the fact is that no useful purpose is served by seeking to weigh the merits of one against those of the other in any formal way. Life is rich and manifold and each medium has a distinctive task to fulfil. When both are working harmoniously together, communication attains a maximum both of range and efficiency.

We may begin then with the Image and the Word as the basic elements in all communication. But man is not satisfied to have a succession of unco-ordinated images presented to his imagination; this does not constitute communication. Nor is he content simply to utter a series of unconnected sounds to his neighbour. Some principle or principles of *order* must be recognised, some regularities and continuities must be established, some way of relating an image or a word to its wider context must be discovered, if man is to find meaning in his universe and a way of communicating this meaning to others. What then are the main principles which operate in the process of combining words and images so that they become efficient agents of communication ?

I suggest that two fundamental operations belong to the very structure of the world in which we live and that these two operations have become entirely characteristic of man himself. I call these operations Building and Sharing. From one point of view the world itself is a marvellous structure built out of particles, atoms, molecules or whatever tiny elements are regarded as the " bricks " of the universe. These bricks are fashioned into shapes and patterns and built up within successive wholes in such a way that the normal image which strikes the human eye at any moment is that of a structure made up of many elemental parts but held together within a visible unity. Even when man uses the telescope or the microscope the image which he sees can be described in much the same way : elemental " bricks " or shapes are *built* together within a surprising unity of shape and form.

But from another point of view the world is a marvellous system of inter-connections in which waves, charges, potentials or whatever tiny forces are regarded as the connecting " links " of the universe, are constantly in motion. These " links " also take on shapes and forms with the result that whenever man's proper receptive organs intercept one of these links a particular pattern of " information " is received from and through it. In other words, the world may be regarded as a supremely wonderful organisation of relationships in which the essential and constant process is that of the "*sharing*" of "information"[1] of all kinds.

Now man himself has tended to conceive his own most important functions and activities in one of these two ways. Looking back, for example, into the life of the ancient world, we find a word in the Egyptian language (KOD) which was used in the most widely varied contexts. It seems to have been originally employed in connection with the potter's craft. By turning his wheel steadily and patiently, he shaped the clay and formed useful and beautiful objects. So KOD meant to turn around, to turn in a circle : then to make pots, to be a potter : then to form, create, build, work : and finally, when used substantively, likeness, image, similarity.[2] From the simple creative activity of making pots the word extended its range until it covered some of the most complicated forms of art and language.

Such a word provides a vivid illustration of one of man's basic "drives" or instincts. He loves to create, to mould the material of his environment into satisfying shapes, to repeat again and again the fabrication of a form which appeals to him in a special way, to compare one article with another, to improve upon his previous performance—in short, to build up, piece by piece, an ever more imposing structure out of a very few basic patterns. And what he tries to do with the clay from the river-bed, he seeks also to do with his words and with his images. To construct a

[1] I am using "information" in the semi-technical sense which has become common in the modern science of communication.
[2] E. Cassirer. *The Philosophy of Symbolic Forms.* p. 288.

symbolic model of the universe in which he dwells is one of the dominant motives inspiring and regulating human activity.

But there is another important and significant " drive." In the Hebrew language two words are constantly associated with one another : they are *KARATH* and *BERITH*. The first has the meanings to cut, to cut off, to divide : the second designates a covenant, the community formed through a covenant, the state of peace and harmony resulting from a covenant, the free interchange of friendly relations within the covenant.[1]

When the two words are used together one main image emerges. It is of man relating himself to his fellow-man, through sharing food, through sharing blood, through sharing possessions, through sharing the particular quality of life which the other lacks. Such a sharing inevitably involves a cutting, a dividing, a separating : followed by a conjunction, a coming together, a connecting of " unlikes " and even opposites. And again what man does with his own peculiar possessions—his life, his breath, his blood, his clothes, his weapons, his food—he does also with his words and with his images. To come together through sharing in some channel of meeting or participation, is the motive force inspiring

[1] The exact terminology of *berith* is still uncertain though many incline to derive it from the root *Barah* 1—to eat with, to establish community with by eating, in which case *karath* would mean to cut off, the reference being to the cutting off of ceremonial food and passing it to the other party at the meal. On the other hand, karath may mean simply to cut, in which case the reference might be to the practice whereby the two parties to the covenant used to cut into each other's flesh and to share, either by contact or by drinking, the blood thus drawn out.

another great section of human activity. Let us now look at these two forms of activity, *building* and *sharing*, more closely.

II.   THE BUILDING PROCESS

The process of building images finds a simple but striking expression when a child is making mud-pies or sketching freely on paper. The child is happier in handling flexible and easily malleable material and in being free to build up its own form than it is in building with prefabricated bricks, however enjoyable the latter process may be. Whether by inheritance from the collective unconscious of mankind or by direct reflection from its own natural and social environment, the child seems already to be in possession of certain fundamental shapes—the circle, the square, and perhaps the sphere and the pyramid—by which it can direct its activities. With the wet sand or with paper and pencil and with these basic geometrical shapes, the great adventure of building begins, an adventure which is to become more and more complex as life goes on. By trial and error, by success and failure, by imitation and origination, by repetition and modification, the experiments go forward, though for a long time the activities of the growing individual are limited by the boundaries of the tiny world in which he seems to be enclosed.

The process of language-building is entirely similar. Nothing is more flexible or more malleable than wind-music. Shapes and patterns of sound are provided by the mouth as it fashions the escaping breath. So with rough or smooth breath as material and with the shapes of mouth and lips as fashioners, the great adventure of building structures of language begins. The same variations of trial and error are involved. Gradually the great organism of a language reproduces itself in the growing individual though in a minute way the language itself may be inflected or modified by the individual in the course of the process.

But there is another important aspect of the building enterprise. Not only does the child love to build its stationary houses and castles and towers : it loves also to build up patterns of *movement*, rhythms of behaviour, and regular habits of activity. He is aware of the movement of life around and he tries to represent it in sketches and paintings and models. In the kind of activity which ordered play or dancing or running or swimming provides he gains an increasing sense of confidence and freedom. So, too, in the growing mastery of language there are runs and movements and sequences which give immediate delight and an increasing sense of power ; they are similar to the rhythmic movements of the several organs which move with unfailing regularity during the life-span of any healthy body.

Here, then, is our first comprehensive picture : a growing and expanding building with rhythmic movements and regular patterns of activity being constantly performed within its context. Symbolically this picture has again and again found outward expression as men have constructed a house of God and performed a regular cycle of cultic activities within it. According to the experience and resources of any particular society so will its sanctuary or temple be. It may be a simple circular mud-hut : it may be a magnificent Sun-temple such as existed in ancient Egypt. Again the interior ritual may consist of a simple daily offering : it may involve ordered priest-hoods with elaborate sacrifices. But however simple or however grandiose it may be, the fundamental principle is the same. Materials are shaped, carved into patterns, fitted together, adjusted, added to one another. Then, within the context of the growing building, which itself constitutes the model of the world-view of the society, a regular cultus is enacted. By this means the society seeks constantly to re-identify itself with the universal life-process on which it depends and of which it forms a part.

But this pattern which is clearly revealed in the history of temple-building and cult-activities finds still wider expression in the history of the growth and development of language. Man not only builds temples, he also builds *myths* : he not only performs sacred actions, he also recites and sings sacred *liturgies*. Just as the temple serves to gather up tentative building experiments already made on a smaller and more temporary scale and integrates them into a central, permanent, over-arching structure which symbolises the world-view of the particular culture : so the myth serves to gather up the word-sequences which have grown out of the ordinary regularities of human experience (birth and death, eating and drinking, mating and childbearing, sowing and reaping) and integrates them into an elaborate, all-comprehending structure which symbolises the same general world-view in words. It is in fact out of the materials provided by images recurring again and again in dreams, together with experiences recurring again and again within the limited circle of the life of a particular society, that the great myth of the society is constructed. And although further experience may in certain respects modify and extend the myth, it will not be radically changed so long as the society maintains its own settled existence within its own limited environment.

So also, in the realm of liturgical creation, just as the sacrificial cultus seeks to gather up the experiments in life-promotion and life-participation made on a small scale (e.g. ceremonies relating to birth and death, fertility-practices of stock-rearing and agricultural societies) and integrates them into one all-inclusive world-renewing rite : so the liturgy of prayer and music combined—the prayer including praises, petitions and thanksgivings and the music covering the whole range of human feeling—seeks to gather up the sound-regularities which man has used in his attempt to adjust himself to his environment and expresses them in a symphony of words and sounds which symbolises the rhythmic beat of the universal life-process. Modifications and amplifications of sacrificial-rite and prayer-liturgy there may be, but once the general structure is established it maintains its stability until through some major encounter the whole character of the society is changed.

I have tried to sketch in a broad way one dominant aspect of the human situation. Man shapes and builds the materials which he finds to hand, the images and patterns which he sees, the tones and variations which he hears. Symbolically his structures appear in the form of temples and cults, of myths and liturgies. Can these structures themselves be regarded as media through which a Divine communication is being made ? Or will a new Divine Image and Word cause new structures to come into existence ? What at least seems clear is that any Divine communication which is to come meaningfully to *man*, must relate itself in some way to these general structures which constitute so important a part of the human situation.

III.   THE PROCESS OF EXCHANGE

The process of *sharing* belongs to a somewhat different phase and aspect of human life. The activity of building is essentially a means of extending the range and outreach of the human personality. There is, as yet, little thought of direct giving and receiving but only of enlarging the self through interaction with the environment. But gradually the realisation dawns that there are other selves who are also creators and possessors. If the society is homogeneous and tightly integrated this recognition need not lead to any serious disturbance. The kinds of buildings which all are constructing, the kinds of rhythms which all are creating, are not likely to be very dissimilar. There is therefore no urgent need for give and take. All are working in the same way to the same end.

But even in a closely-knit society tensions and conflicts may arise, especially between age-groups and between the sexes. Still more, when a society consisted of small family groups or of clans scattered over wide stretches of country, often on the move, often subject to violent experiences, with certain groups meeting situations of which the others have no knowledge, periodically encountering tribes of strange customs and language : occasions of friction, of estrangement, of divergent experiences, are bound to occur. At best, one group may prove fortunate in securing useful goods or valuable materials of some kind : at worst, a group may encounter misfortune and fail to discover sufficient food or water for daily needs.

Whatever the nature of the experiences of these mobile groups and clans may be, one thing is clear. The outstanding events in life are those associated with *meeting* and *encounter*. To confront an animal which is the object of the chase, to stumble upon a water-hole, to discover a new kind of terrain, to meet a stranger—these are experiences of unusual significance. Immediately some form of hospitality or interchange becomes possible. If food has been obtained through a successful hunt that must be shared with fellow-kinsmen : if a new source of water has been found, others must be given the opportunity of tasting the fresh stream : if a new weapon has been discovered, its efficiency must be demonstrated when circumstances allow. Most important of all, there must from time to time be a general assembly to which all the kinsmen can come, each bringing his own gift and receiving in turn some article needed for his own or his family's good.

But what is true of general experience is true also of the development of imagery and language. There comes a stage when an increasing command of shape and sound depends not so much upon imitation and repetition as upon the challenge of new situations and the sharpness of dialectical interchange. To express in mime one's reaction to a sudden and unexpected event, to be confronted by a radically different opinion from one's own and to attempt to justify oneself through words, to grapple with the implications of a completely unknown language system—these are experiences which stimulate altogether new experiments in the use of imagery and language and on occasion lead to exciting new discoveries.

But again in the normal way of things man is not content to keep such a discovery to himself. He brings his newly-fashioned image, his unusual metaphor, his striking paradox, and offers it to his fellows for their consideration. In return he is prepared to listen to them and to receive picture-gifts for his own enrichment. One of the simplest examples of this process is the joke, a form of speech which depends for its effectiveness almost entirely upon the element of surprise, upon the creation of tension and its sudden relaxation. There is nothing that a man is more anxious to share with his fellows than a good joke. He may chuckle over it himself for a short while, but then he must pass it on to another or its pungency diminishes and is ultimately lost. Through person to person meetings and through the symbolical re-enacting of meetings imagery and language gain new life and leap forward in surprising ways.

Our second main picture, then, is that of a richly variegated assembly, composed of those of dissimilar and often of contradictory backgrounds and experiences, drawn together on a particular occasion for the primary purpose of inter-relationship and interchange. Such assemblies have played no small part in human history in the fields of commerce (the market), culture (the university) and politics (the parliament). Normally the assembly does not convene in a purely haphazard way but adopts a definite procedure whereby, amidst all the give-and-take of ordinary encounters, place is found for some occasion of a central and representative character through which the particular purpose of the meeting can be dramatically set forth. At all gatherings of this kind objects of value and experiences of interest are given and received.

Symbolically this picture has again and again found expression in human history when men have convened at a chosen place (often associated with some significant historical event) and have there engaged in dialectical exercises of a religious character. The occasion may have been yearly, monthly, or weekly. The place may have been a simple enclosure, a wayside chapel or a vast auditorium. The exercises may have consisted in a simple interchange of testimonies, through recital or through prayer : in a dialectical interchange between a leader and the rest of the company as he acts and speaks and they respond : in an interchange of sacramental symbols (sacrificial meat, bread or wine) in a common feast : in an interchange of special insignia (a robe, a ring or an amulet) in dramatic gesture and song. But whatever its form the underlying principle is the same : men and women, having some common bond through race or kinship or historical event, yet scattered abroad and exposed to wide variations of experience, feel impelled to come together from time to time so that in a renewal of intercourse each may enrich the other and a new social harmony may be established. Further, within this assembly a dramatic representation of interchange is normally enacted so that the central purpose of the whole assembly may be sealed and confirmed.

In the general development of imagery and language the form which corresponds to the corporate assembly is the *social history* : pictures and words are brought together and related to one another, reports are sifted and criticised and so history is created and expanded, corrected and enriched. Just as the corporate assembly brings together all sorts and conditions of men—men who have been moulded by varying and often surprising experiences—so *history* brings together within one assembly of words and images all sorts and conditions of testimonies by which these experiences have been recorded : and just as within the assembly the exercise of dialectic is the means by which enlargement and enrichment is gained, so history itself constantly advances as the coming together of new discoveries and new criticisms makes the already existent formulation in some respects inadequate. Through the meeting of past and present, of the familiar with the unfamiliar, of the report with the criticism, of the witness with the cross-examination, history lives and thrives. History in fact may be regarded as the meeting-ground of the dramas and pictures and stories and traditions of a particular section of human society : every new formulation of this history is of value so long as it leaves room for a continuing dialectic between the new and the old, and even for the revolutionary change which some new discovery may involve.

Here then is another dominant aspect of the human situation. Man is not content to remain for ever within the circumscribed and the well known. He stretches out towards new adventures and new encounters. His eyes are fascinated by strange sights, his ears are captivated by unusual sounds. Symbolically the give-and-take of new experience is focused in the solemn assembly where dramatic interchange takes place, while in the realm of cultural development the ongoing process of the writing and recording of history provides the model of this particular aspect of the human situation. Again the question arises as to whether these patterns of human experience can be regarded as the actual media of a

Divine communication ? Or will a new Divine Image and Word disclose themselves to man in some other way ? At least it must be said again that any Divine communication which seems to have no reference to these characteristic ways by which man has handled his own images and words will have little chance of entering meaningfully into the human situation.

CHAPTER THREE

God's Image and God's Word

I. THE OLD TESTAMENT

So far I have focused attention upon two pairs which seem to me to be of the highest significance in the development of individual and social life. The Image and the Word are of vital importance in all processes of human communication. The activities of Building and Sharing constantly enlarge and extend the range of man's communication through sight and through sound. I propose now to examine the records and testimonies of the Christian tradition and to ask how, according to this tradition, God has communicated Himself to men and how this communication, when given, has been transmitted from man to man and from generation to generation. In the main I shall be concerned not so much with asking whether the Christian claim is valid or not but rather with ascertaining what in fact this claim really is.

In the first place it is worth pointing out that the Bible as a whole has no interest in what might be called impersonal or purely automatic communications. There is no suggestion of coded information miraculously let down from heaven (perhaps the

41

nearest approach to such a conception is that of the two tables of the Law : but these, we are told, were actually transcribed by a person Moses) or of miraculous operations on earth set going by a direct Divine impulse (even such a phenomenon as the vision of the burning bush is not unrelated to man's other experiences within the natural order). Communications which produce highly abnormal human reactions—seizures, frenzies, babblings—are suspect : those connected with trances or with some form of clairvoyance exercise no major influence. It is possible to affirm that the Bible's whole concern is with communications to the eye and ear of man : it is what men have seen, what they have heard, that is of central importance.

But do men really see Divine forms and shapes ? Do they really hear Divine commands and messages ? What, for example, is the witness of the Old Testament ? Perhaps the most characteristic feature of this witness is the emphasis laid upon the *word* of God rather than upon the visual manifestation of God. In the light of what we know of the Hebrew manner of life, this is not surprising. For traditionally he was a man of the uplands and the open spaces, a nomad with a deep-seated suspicion of settled city life, though eager to meet with his fellow-clansmen on set occasions for mutual interchange and encouragement. It was on these occasions that oral " testimonies " were recited and a solemn feast enjoyed and the way prepared for the gradual collection of the stories

which was in course of time to become the history
of the people of God.

In the normal habitat of the Hebrew there was
little variety in the " seen." Few startling impressions
came to him through his eyes. But he was ever on the
alert to listen. The cries of the birds and the voices
of the beasts, the murmur of peaceable conversation
and the shout of alarm, the rhythm of the chant and
the sharpness of the command—all these were familiar
to him. In fact, the channels of sound were for him
the all-important channels of communication. What
could be more natural, then, than that he should
describe an overwhelming urgency of constraint, an
irresistible impulsion from beyond, as a *word* from
the Lord ? It was like a fire burning within that had
to find outlet, it was like a heavy weight pressing
down and demanding release : the communication from beyond found its outlet in *words*, and
these words—rich in variety though constant in
their witness to Divine judgment and grace—were
confessed and acknowledged as words from God
Himself.

Yet communication to sight was not entirely lack-
ing. As I have suggested, to the ancient nomads
there was normally little variety in the " seen." But
even in the natural order there was the sudden flash
of the lightning, the unexpected eruption of the
volcano, the strange phenomenon of the eclipse.
Still more, when the nomad began to be drawn into
the vortex of civilised life and began to feel the
powerful pressures emanating from well organised

societies, historical events began to take on a highly dramatic significance for him. When disaster befell him, he beheld the judgments of *God* abroad in the earth : when a great deliverance came, he believed that he had seen the manifestation of the glory and power of *God*. In other words it was through the extraordinary phenomenon of nature, it was through the startling conjunctions of events in history, that the Hebrew saw the operation of transcendent forces, *saw*, according to his own confession, the glory of God. The mighty deeds which he saw with his own eyes and later celebrated through ritual forms, were to him outward and visible communications of the activity of the living God Himself.

These are the leading emphases of the prophetic writings of the Old Testament and of the most creative period of Israel's history. At the same time there is good evidence that the Hebrew forefathers originally came out of a more settled community-life which possessed a well defined world-picture expressed in myth and symbol and ritual form. The general structure of this world-picture remained in the background of the consciousness of the Israelite community and when at length a more settled culture began to form in Palestine and when new contacts began to be made with the established sanctuaries and the developed mythologies of the surrounding civilisations, a distinctive Jewish interpretation of the universe gradually took shape.

This was expressed through temple and myth and, while the framework owed much to older pagan

influences, its wholehearted acknowledgement of the
image and word of Yahweh was creatively new. The
firmament revealed the handiwork of Yahweh but
Yahweh did not dwell *within* either His creation or
its symbolic form, the Temple. The regularities of
the heavenly bodies proclaimed the word of Yahweh
but Yahweh's activities were not limited either by
these patterns of the created order or by their mythical
representation.[1]

In this late period of Jewish history two characteristic sets of forms are to be seen side by side,
often in somewhat uneasy relation to one another.
There are on the one side the prophetic stories and
the prophetic oracles of criticism, gathered together
to constitute the *sacred history*; these are closely
associated with the feasts of solemn *assembly* at which
selected passages from the sacred history were recited
and applied to the contemporary situation. On the
other side there is the *temple*, passing through many
vicissitudes, but at times of relative settlement providing the locus for the regular offering of sacrifice;
this is the setting of the growing *myth* which regards
Jerusalem and its Temple as the centre of the whole
universe and elaborates it through the regular recita-
tion of psalmody and prayer. These are the forms
which took shape in Israel, first in its period of
relative isolation, then in its period of close association with other peoples. What then was the bond
which held them together?

---

[1] The general conclusions of these paragraphs are, I believe, supported
at various points by Dr. Harold Fisch's interesting article, "The Analogy
of Nature," in J.T.S., October, 1955.

The only final bond which no strain of history was
able to break was the stubborn conviction that the
living God, Yahweh, had chosen and called and
saved and guided this particular people, Israel, from
first to last. Their history was essentially the history
of *God's* activity : their assemblies were primarily
for the purpose of celebrating the mighty acts of *God*.
And it was because of the conviction that God had
brought them to the land of Canaan and given them
Jerusalem as their fortress, that it became possible to
think of God's activity being focused in and emanating
from Mount Zion : it became natural for them to
regard their sacrificial system as designed to maintain
in constant rhythmical movement a vital communion
with God Himself. There was always the danger that
the living God would become a mere figure within
the national history or a mere force within the national
mythology. But so long as men confessed that it was
God Who had redeemed their fathers out of the house
of bondage, so long as they confessed that it was
God Who in the beginning had created the heavens
and the earth, so long was it possible for these two
sides of Israel's life to be held together within a
living relationship.

Thus the Old Testament bears witness to dramatic
events in history where men *saw* the mighty hand of
God at work : it also describes the original Creation
and the Temple of Jerusalem, each in its own way
revealing the pattern of the Divine providence. Again
it bears witness to prophetic oracles of judgment and
grace through which men *heard* the word of the

Lord : it also records the laws and psalms through
which priestly interpreters described the ordered
rhythms and regularities of God's universe. The Old
Testament provides in fact a wonderful collection of
formal images and word patterns. But they lack a
true integrating agent. It also supplies a vivid series
of lively oracles and dramatic events. But they wait
for a true personal fulfilment. *The* Image has yet to
be revealed : *the* Word has yet to be spoken.

II.   THE NEW TESTAMENT

Two sublime proclamations of the New Testament
reveal the nature of the new communication which
has been made to mankind through the historic mission
of Jesus the Christ. " God, Who commanded the
light to shine out of darkness, hath shined in our
hearts to give the light of the knowledge of the glory
of God in the face of Jesus Christ." Here is the
Light which integrates all other lights ; here is the
most expressive revelation of the image ever to be
communicated to human eyes. And again : " God,
Who at sundry times and in divers manners spoke in
time past unto the fathers through the prophets, has,
at the end of these days, spoken unto us through His
Son." Here is the Word which fulfils all other words :
here is the most important " information " ever to
be communicated to human ears. He is the image
of the God Who had never been seen by mortal eye.
He is the Word of the God Whose actual voice had
never been heard by mortal ear.

But while these affirmations give a striking emphasis
to the Image on the one hand and to the Word on
the other, no too sharply defined distinctions must
be made between the two. " God·has spoken through
His Son "—but the writer goes on immediately to
declare that the Son is the outshining of God's glory
and the authentic image of His eternal nature. " God
has shined in our hearts to give the Light "—but the
light has just been called " good news " and it was
as the direct result of the command of God that the
light first shone out from the darkness. Gospel and
light, word and image, are inextricably bound together
in the Christian revelation.

Yet we may consider each in turn, seeking to see
how these and other similar testimonies of the New
Testament are related to the human senses of sight
and hearing. Taking first the word (the major
emphasis of the New Testament as well as of the Old),
the writer of the Epistle to the Hebrews declares
emphatically that the word spoken through the Son
is not independent of the many communications
transmitted to the fathers through the prophets. In
other words, there are *patterns of language* already
available. A vocabulary, a grammar, a syntax, in the
widest sense of the terms, have been gradually built
up during the long period in which a people's recurring experiences of the providence of God (giving
patterns of regularity) were intermingled with signal
examples of His judgment and salvation (giving
creatively new developments). Such a word as
" Son," for example, is neither commonplace nor

radically new. It is a word whose history can be traced through the Old Testament record, now applied to the experience of the people of God in their organic relationship to the Father Who has adopted them as His own, now applied to a heroic individual called by God to fulfil His special purpose. The word " Christ " again had come to be applied not only to the people in their continuing corporate mission as God's anointed servants but also to the Divine Hero Who would break through existing patterns and forms and inaugurate the reign of God. Or yet again, such a word as " redemption " has the background both of repeated and relatively familiar experiences of the manumission of slaves, and also of critical and determinative deliverances of quite out-standing historical significance, such as the Exodus from Egypt and the later Return from Exile. Into the midst of this dialectical language-pattern the living and incarnate Word of God ultimately comes, and the New Testament is, in effect, the result, in words, of this unique event.

What, then, are the main features of the emerging pattern of communication ? Traditionally a useful distinction has been made between the *Person* of Christ and the *Work* of Christ, and although this distinction can easily be exaggerated yet it corresponds to the great importance which the New Testament gives on the one hand to the *Names* of Christ and on the other to the descriptions of what He *achieved* in the realm of the relations between God and man.

First let us look at His *Names*.[1] These are derived almost entirely from the language-cradle of the Old Testament, though in the case of such titles as Word and Lord the reference to the distinctively Greek language-cradle begins to be seen. It may indeed be said that whereas the name " Christ " gathers up into itself one vast section of the historical experience of the Hebrews, the name " Logos " (Word) later gathers up a similar vast section of the historical experience of the Greeks. To confess the crucified and risen Jesus of Nazareth as Christ, Son of God, Son of Man, Son of David, Servant of God, Wisdom of God, Word of God, King of Kings, Lord of Lords—is to confess that God has spoken through a Person Who rightly assumes each of these particular Names and yet at the same time re-makes the Name in the very process of doing so. He can assume it because an established name encodes within one concentrated form a multitude of communications which have worked themselves into the accumulated experience of a particular society : He re-makes it because the communication expressed through His own person bursts the bounds of every existent form through which it has been transmitted. Thus through the great *Names* of the New Testament—names which men in the power of the eternal Spirit felt compelled to ascribe to Jesus of Nazareth—the witness of God to His Son has been communicated to mankind in determinate form. What still remains

[1] For the importance of these names see Vincent Taylor. *The Names of Jesus.*

is for every language and every culture to bring its
own archetypal names and offer them to God so that
in the process of being ascribed to the same Jesus of
Nazareth they may be re-made by the same process
of Divine alchemy.

What now of His Work, His final achievement?
Again the descriptions are taken almost entirely from
the more dynamic language forms of the Old Testament, though " reconciliation " and " glorification "
may approach nearer to the characteristic world-view
of Hellenism. Through His death and resurrection,
it was proclaimed, Jesus had *redeemed* them from all
unrighteousness, had *saved* them from their sins, had
forgiven them all their iniquities, had inaugurated a
new *covenant*, had brought them home to God. Here
the verbs indicative of the revolutionary change are
taken over from the Hebrew background but the
reference of the change is altered. The vocabulary
which had been formulated mainly as a result of
experiences in the world of material conditions and
physical change is now applied to a supreme achievement in the world of moral values and spiritual
change. So, later, in the Greek world a vocabulary
which had been developed within the realms of
æsthetic and intellectual experience was taken over and
applied to a critical change in the world of personal
and moral relationships. In fact, through the great
Atonement words of the New Testament—words
which men in the power of the living Spirit applied
to the mighty work achieved by Jesus in death and
resurrection—the witness of God to the new era

inaugurated by His Servant has been communicated to men in determinate form. Again, however, it remains for every tribe and tongue to bring its own word of radical change and offer it to God so that it may be transformed within the new creative association.

The primary appeal of the New Testament is to the word. Yet the faculty of sight is never ignored, and in some parts of the communicating process it is regarded as of major importance. In the normal way of things, before men attribute a name to a person, especially a name which crystallises into one word a character revealed over a period of time, they need to *see*. They watch the person's behaviour in varying situations, they observe correspondences to that quality or sum of qualities which the name implies, they take note of continuities and repetitions in the career of the person on whom their interest is focused, and at length, as in the case of the famous confession at Cæsarea Philippi,[1] the identification is daringly made. It is true that reports that men hear, especially if they are vividly and imaginatively told, can be of great value in estimating the significance of a career and identifying it by name. Nevertheless, nothing can quite take the place of actual *seeing*. The report goes out : " We have found Him of whom Moses and the Prophets did write," and when the sceptic asks whether any good thing can come out of Nazareth the response is immediately : " Come and *see*."

[1] Mark 8, 29. " And Peter answereth and saith ... Thou art the Christ."

In the main these New Testament identifications are made against the background of the career-patterns provided by the Old Testament. A notable example is that of the Servant of Isaiah 40-55. In these chapters some of the most vivid pen-portraits of the Old Testament are to be found. Probably they were painted by an artist who had the experiences of an actual individual or community in mind. Even so they constitute a rich interpretation rather than a direct representation and provide a wonderful career-pattern for the use of those who were seeking to bear witness to that which had been revealed to them through the Person of Jesus of Nazareth. They had seen Him in His relations with the common people, in His deeds of mercy, in His suffering and passion, in His death and resurrection. He did not strive nor cry neither was His voice heard shouting in the streets : the bruised reed He did not break neither did He quench the smoking flax : He had borne the sick-nesses and infirmities of the weak and distressed : He had been led as a lamb to the slaughter : He had been numbered with the transgressors and had made His grave with the wicked. Surely this was the true *Servant of God* through whom it had pleased God to fulfil His mighty purpose. Seeing Him against these vivid backgrounds—the Christ, the Servant, the Son of Man : perhaps, too, the Son of David, the Priest after the order of Melchizedek, the Shepherd—they made the daring identifications of faith and acclaimed Him as the One whose face, whose character, unveiled the very knowledge of the glory of God Himself.

In the case of the *work* of Christ the visual medium is less immediately appropriate. The sudden event, the revolutionary change, cannot so easily be captured by the eye. It is possible to recognise that a transformation has taken place within a whole situation : formerly it was that way, now it is this way. But the actual observation of the transforming event may be confined to a very few. Indeed even the few observers who are on the watch may not be certain of the exact nature of the change that has undoubtedly taken place. They see suffering declining to death : they see new life advancing towards a future glory : but the precise moment of the great reversal they have not seen. They speak with their tongues the wonderful works of God and seek through widening experiences to find language forms which can more adequately declare the nature of the Divine intervention.

But so far as seeing is concerned, it must chiefly be an observation of context—the state of things beforehand, the state of things afterwards. Reflecting on their own experience and on the experience of the world at large, men see that whereas there was darkness now there is light, whereas there was the bondage of slavery now there is the expansiveness of freedom, whereas there was chaos and disorder now there is harmony and purpose. But the crisis itself was not open to outward vision nor is it describable in visual terms. He redeemed us, He justified us, He reconciled us—by such words, drawn, it is true, from the context of deep personal experience, men have borne witness to the universal ·significance of the saving

work of Christ.   The good news of this so great
deliverance, as is usually the case with reports of lesser
deliverances in human history, is communicated by
words which men speak and hear.

III.   "WE HAVE SEEN, WE HAVE HEARD"

God's Image appeared in human form and men saw
Him in a wide variety of visual situations : God's
Word was spoken through the events of a human
career and men heard Him in a succession of dialectical encounters.   These innumerable secondary
images and words, each constituting a partial communication of the full-orbed Divine Image or of the
critical Divine Word, needed to be built up and
co-ordinated for further transmission.   In large
measure the New Testament is the result of this
double process.

Let us look first at the co-ordination of words.
We read of Jesus calling certain men to be with Him
in order that they might hear His words and engage
in a continuing master-disciple dialectic : we read of
assemblies gathering to listen to His stories and later
having fellowship with one another in His Name :
we read of the house-churches of the Mediterranean
world where the early Christians came together on
the Lord's Day to share with one another the broken
bread and the verbal testimonies to the common
Saviour and Lord.   Through the interchange which
these assemblies promoted and encouraged, stories,
dialogues, testimonies, letters—all in some way con-

cerned with the reconciling work of the Son of God
—gradually came together to form the new *history* of
the people of God. This history, centering in Jesus,
brought together past and present, present and
future : Jew and Gentile, bond and free : grace and
judgment, holiness and sinfulness : all to find their
place of meeting and meaning in Him. Of the forms
of assembly the most characteristic was that in which
the interchange of words culminated in the interchange of bread and wine in a common meal. In the
breaking of the bread and the sharing of the fruit of
the vine, the covenant which sealed the togetherness
of God and man in Christ was constantly renewed.
Of the forms of speech the most characteristic were
the parable and the story, the parable bearing witness
in a graphic way to the general effects of the entry of
God's kingdom into human affairs—the story telling
what actually did happen when Jesus, the agent of
God's Kindgom, came amongst men.

But although these patterns of *sharing* provide the
primary setting of the New Testament they are not
all-inclusive. A *building* process was also taking
place. There is the outline-sketch of a *temple* with its
appropriate liturgy : the beginnings of a *myth* with
its appropriate language forms. Amongst the charges
brought against Jesus in the court of the high-priest,
one was almost certainly founded upon an authentic
saying of His, even though it may have been misunderstood and misrepresented. In some way He
had spoken about the destruction of the Jerusalem
temple and of the erecting of a new sanctuary, the

sanctuary, says the Fourth Evangelist, of His Body.
And this basic conception is taken up and developed
in other writings of the New Testament. While calling
men to be with Him and fashioning them into a band
of witnesses to the Kingdom, Jesus was also building
a temple, a temple which was mysteriously comparable
to a growing body. This Body gathered men and
women together into a rich complex of organic
relationships and the rhythm of its continuing life-
flow was maintained as they offered sacrifices of praise
and thanksgiving to God through Him.

As regards the *myth*, the centre from which imagery
and language stretch out to embrace the whole
universe is no longer the rock of Jerusalem but the
rock which is Christ. He is the Pattern through
Whom, in the beginning, the universe came into
existence : He is the Power through Whom the
universe expands towards its God-appointed destiny.
Furthermore, the language forms which constitute
the rhythmic regularities of the myth are the analogies,
the types, the allegories, the mystery-dramas—all
bearing witness to the sacrificial nature of the Divine
life—such as may be found in many parts of the
New Testament but more particularly in the Fourth
Gospel. The most characteristic form of the liturgy
of the new Temple-Body is the *spiritual sacrifice*.
(This may be externalised in the eucharist but not
exclusively so.) The most characteristic forms of
ordered speech and imagery within the myth are the
analogy and the mystery-drama, the analogy showing
in general terms (Jesus as the Light, the Way, the

True Vine), the mystery-drama through specific examples (the changing of water into wine, the bringing of sight to the man born blind, the raising of Lazarus to life), how the eternal life of God has flowed into the world and back again to the Father through the Son.

Let me try to sum up the conclusions of this chapter. It has become clear that the earliest Christian witnesses expressed their essential testimony in two forms : " We have seen," " We have heard." The innumerable images which they had seen were first brought together and builded together to form the great Name-portraits of the New Testament. In most instances rough sketches, as it were, were already available as the result of dramatic experiences of the people of God recorded in the Old Testament Scriptures. Yet such names as Christ, Servant, Lamb of God, were not taken over without adaptation and even re-creation. Rather it was because of what men had seen in and through Jesus of Nazareth that the new and distinctive portrait gallery of *Names* appeared in the New Testament, Names which each in its own way depict the impression made by Jesus upon those who companied with Him.

Further, the innumerable words which they had heard became encoded or concentrated within short and vivid testimonies which may be called Atonement short-proclamations : " Christ died for our sins," " the redemption that is in Christ Jesus," " being justified by His blood." Again these forms are not entirely new for in every case some decisive event or pattern

of events in the history of Israel has served to supply
the elements of the imagery and vocabulary employed.
But it was the altogether critical event of the Death
and Resurrection of Jesus of Nazareth which had
changed, so these witnesses believed, the universal
situation of estrangement between God and man
and thereby had made possible a universal reconciliation.

If, now, this sketch of God's self-communication
to man be in any way correct it means that we can
answer the questions asked in chapter two by saying
that according to the witness of the Bible *God did not
ignore or despise the structures of communication which
had already come into existence within the course of human
development.* The Divine Image is expressed *through*
the already existing media of human communication
even though no single integration of these media
can be regarded as the fully adequate reproduction
of the Image : the Divine Word is sent forth *through*
already existing media even though again no single
proclamation can be regarded as the final formulation
of the Word. Even God has been willing so to reveal
Himself within the human scene that the images and
the words, the names and the proclamations which
have come to birth within the universal history of
mankind could become the fitting vehicles for man
to bear his testimony to what he had seen and heard.

Moreover, the process of communication can
never be regarded as complete. God is still communicating Himself through images and through
words which transmit the definitive revelation in

Christ to later places and times. In the New Testament, in fact, the material is already to hand for the expansive building enterprise and the far-extending communicating operation which constitute the very life and task of the Christian Church. The Names are to be so integrated with one another and so related to new environments that they will come to form a three-dimensional model of a growing Divine Organism (the Temple of His Body), an organism in and through which the Divine Life flows out into ever-expanding areas of the world's existence and gathers them up into their true place of healing and sanctification within the continuing self-oblation of the Son of God. In addition the Atonement-proclamations are to be so related to one another and to alien organised systems of world-relationships (as expressed, for example, in language systems) that they come to form a dynamic model, a model which may be described as the continuing dialectic of a Divine Covenant. This dialectic is such that ever new reconciliations are being effected as God's Word of Judgment and Grace in Jesus Christ meets and challenges and saves the alienated elements of the universal life of mankind. It is this dual process of the growth of the Temple-Building and the extension of the Covenant-Relationship that we are to see illustrated in the historical development which I shall describe in the next two chapters.

CHAPTER FOUR

The Beginnings
of Christian Communication

I. THE GOSPEL AND THE HEBRAIC TRADITION

GOD'S COMMUNICATION to mankind, the New Testament claims, was made through a particular person at a particular time in a particular place. This particular time was intimately connected with a far longer period of history—the history of a particular people whose essential experiences are recorded in the Old Testament scriptures. The particular place was intimately connected with a far wider area of country—the area in which those essential experiences had occurred. Even the particular person was intimately connected with a far wider society—the particular people whose language, whose traditions, whose manner of life he inherited. This means that by no possible process known to man can the essential communication be extracted, as it were, from its given setting, and transferred, with no traces of its original expression in humanity clinging to it, to another setting in time and space. The process of translating and transposing is far more complex, and

I shall try in the next two chapters to examine some of the factors involved in the task.

I have suggested that God's communication was made both to ear and eye.[1] What Jesus *was*, in the pattern of His character, could make a special appeal to the eye. The news of what Jesus *did*, in the crisis of death and resurrection, could make a special appeal to the ear. The patterns of His character are crystallised in the great *names* of the New Testament : the witness to His saving work is concentrated in the great *atonement words* of the New Testament. Moreover, the pattern of His character is reflected into the future both through the pattern of the life of the Christian community and through symbolic visual images : the witness to His saving work is relayed into the future both through the actual proclamation of the good news and through symbolic verbal forms. The all-important question now is how this pattern and this witness are to be communicated into new cultures whose images and speech-patterns are vastly different from those of the culture within which the communication was originally made and into which it was first of all reflected and relayed.

Fortunately the New Testament itself contains material of outstanding importance for the answering of this question. The first major transposition which

---

[1] An early witness could claim not only that he had heard and seen with his eyes but also that his hands had *touched* the word of life : but immediately afterwards, in speaking of his own transmission of the communication, he confines himself to what has been seen and heard (I John 1 1-4). I do not minimise the importance of the senses of touch, taste, and smell, and I recognise the power of communication exercised by the impact of a whole personality. At the same time in the communication of *news* (and the Christian Gospel is " good news ") eye and ear are of altogether primary importance.

Christian missionaries had to make was from the Jewish cultural milieu to the Greek. Their starting-point was the Jewish culture, in which the word occupied the place of eminence and in which the assembly for the exchange of words was the characteristic social pattern. Their basic words and images, moreover, were derived from periods of constant movement and change in the life of the nation, though more regular cycles and sequences had established themselves during the later religious history of the Jews.

In the case of Jesus himself, and indeed of the earliest Christian witnesses, patterns of words and images were employed which were reminiscent of the earlier dynamic phase of Hebrew culture. The parables and stories He told, the dramatic works (acted parables) which He performed, were closely related to the archetypal images and language forms belonging to the heroic and prophetic era of His people's history. The coming together of past and future in the present inbreaking of the Kingdom of God, the achievement of the central work of deliverance which had been foreshadowed in the notable deliverances of the people of God from their enemies, the simultaneous confession of Jesus as Messiah and Suffering Servant—these all belong to the *prophetic* tradition of words and images, being derived from a form of existence of which the characteristic notes were movement, crisis, tribulation, joyful release, judgment, salvation. A history largely composed of dialectical encounters provided an appropriate vocabulary for the description of a mission whose primary objective was to bring man into a critical encounter with God Himself.

But what was to happen when the Gospel began to reach those whose outlook had been modified and even transformed by the influence of Greek culture? What was to happen when it had to be communicated into circles whose whole pattern of life and thought had been moulded by this tradition? In brief, the answer seems to be that whereas the imagery and language forms belonging to the heroic periods of Israel's culture were not abandoned, those of later and more settled Judaism, those of the Judaism which had been more influenced by the great cultures of the Middle East, were made the vehicles for the transposing of God's Word and God's Image into this altogether different culture.

This process would have been exceedingly difficult to carry through had it not been that the Old Testament scriptures had already been translated into the Greek language by representatives of later Jewry, that some at least of the early Christian missionaries had grown up in a Greek environment, and that efforts were already being made to transpose some of the leading Jewish categories into Greek terms, particularly in Alexandria. Nevertheless, the task was immense, for in many respects the prophetic categories seemed to be clean contrary to all for which Greek culture stood. In this new culture the image occupied the place of eminence, the magnificent temple was the characteristic social archetype.

Its basic words and images, though derived in many cases from remote heroic periods of invasion and conquest, had been moulded through centuries of a settled cultural existence to represent abiding forms and patterns in nature and society. No word was more characteristic than *Logos* itself, representing as it did the principle of order in the visible universe corresponding to an identical principle of order in man himself. No image was more typical than that of *the body*, this being used as a striking analogy in relation both to the political society and to the physical universe. How could the communication be made into such an environment?

An examination of the Epistles of St. Paul and of the Johannine writings, reveals clearly that the language and imagery is very largely taken from Rabbinic Judaism, from Alexandrian Judaism, or from Hellenism itself.[1] And it is scarcely possible to read the Epistle to the Hebrews without being transported first into the world of priestly Judaism and then into the world of Platonic dualism. In short, it is the words and images of late priestly Judaism which form the bridge by which the Gospel could move over into the world of Greek culture.

What then are the archetypal images and key-words to be found in Rabbinic Judaism, in Hellenistic Judaism (particularly in Philo) and in the wider fields

[1] The high importance of such a book as W. D. Davies's *Paul and Rabbinic Judaism* is to show that the Apostle was indebted to a vast extent to the world of the Rabbis for his language forms and patterns of thought. No one has shown more clearly than C. H. Dodd, in " The Interpretation of the Fourth Gospel," how the leading themes of the Gospel were already of outstanding importance in the world of Hellenistic Judaism.

of Hellenism and Gnosticism ? First and foremost, all were concerned with the universe as a whole—how it came into existence, how it was sustained. In a general way it was assumed by all that there must have been a model of the universe in the mind of the Creator and this model was conceived in two dominant ways—as a building and as a construction expressed in words. Particularly in Jewish circles the tabernacle or temple was regarded as a direct representation of the universe and the most elaborate schemes were worked out to show how the furniture, the dress of the priests, the vessels of the service, all corresponded to particular parts of the created order.[1] In Philo the process of creation is described in an appealing way : " God, assuming as God would assume, that a beautiful copy could never come into existence without a beautiful model . . . when He willed to create this visible world, first blocked out the intelligible world, in order that using an incorporeal and godlike model he might make the corporeal world."[2]   But this incorporeal model was identified with the Logos and the idea of a construction in *words* clearly emerges.

This concept of the model employed in the creation of the universe is elaborated in a rich variety of ways. The Logos of God is *the Wisdom of God* : in other words, the conception and the expression in words are identical. The Logos is *the Image of God*, His seal stamped upon creation : in other words, the conception and the structure itself are identical.   Still

---

[1] Cp. B. F. Westcott. *The Epistle to the Hebrews*, 238.
[2] Quoted C. H. Dodd. *The Interpretation of the Fourth Gospel*, 67.

more significant, the Logos is *the Son of God*: in some sense the spoken word and the created universe and indeed the temple, each in its own way, can be regarded as the offspring of God. But this leads to further ideas of a heavenly Man and of the universe as comparable to the body of this archetypal Man. Word, Wisdom, Image, Seal, Son, Man, Temple, Body—these are some of the creative concepts or archetypal images which were circulating in the Mediterranean world as men sought to build up their myth of creation. And the distinctive mark of the writings emanating from the more meditative and speculative circles of Judaism, where these were in any way in contact with the world of Hellenism, was their bold and persistent claim that their own Torah, the whole revelation of God made to Israel, could in fact be identified with these various descriptions of the creative principle of the universe. By the Torah of Yahweh the heavens and the earth had been made and it was therefore possible to regard the Torah as the Word of God, the Wisdom of God and even as the Son of God.

When it came to the description of the process by which the universe was sustained, upheld and carried forward, the dual imagery was again employed though not perhaps in so striking a fashion as in the myth of the original creation. Within the tabernacle or temple imagery, elaborate parallels were worked out between the High-Priest in his office and the regularities and stabilities of the universe. Through his offering the world is lifted up to God (Philo declares that when the High-Priest enters the sanctuary to make the prayers and sacrifices of the fathers all the world enters with him) : through the constant re-enactment of the ceremony of reconciliation the unhindered flow of universal life is assured. But then the High-Priest is also to be identified with the Logos, who, in Philo's words " holds together and administers the whole " (universe). He as High-Priest, Logos, Son, Image, sustains and upholds the universe : yet in another sense He is the one who is offered, the body which constitutes the offering, the Logos which in various forms of prayer and praise rises to God. This all implies that the regular, life-sustaining processes of the universe may be conceived either as the rhythmical offering of sacrifice or as the regular offering of words : both the material-order and the language-order provide the High-Priest of the universe with offerings by which he can constantly hold together and administer the whole.

These, then, were some of the images and language-forms available in the Hellenistic world of the first century. In spite of serious hesitations on the part of conservative Jews, many of whom were averse even to translating the Old Testament into Greek, the process of making a bridge from Judaism to Hellenism had been going steadily on. The structure and symbolism of the Old Testament myth had been compared at many points with that of the Hellenistic world. Only—and this is of the highest importance —whereas in the Hellenistic world the transparent sphere through which the whole universe was viewed was the *rational* principle (the Logos), displayed and revealed in the visible environment, in the Jewish world it was the *religious* principle (the Torah), revealed in the record of all Yahweh's dealings with His people. If this major transposition from Logos to Torah could be made at the heart of things, it became possible for the Hellenist to move over into the Jewish religion without leaving behind all the images and language-forms with which he had been familiar. The great question was : Could the early Christians, by using the bridge which was already in process of construction, carry forward the enterprise and bring it to a more successful conclusion than was possible within the limits by which Judaism was inherently bound ?. .

II. THE GOSPEL AND THE GREEKS

Returning now to the three early Christian evangelists to whom I originally referred, it appears that Paul's main work was amongst groups of Gentiles who had had some contact with Judaism, a Judaism moreover which was of a Rabbinic rather than of a prophetic kind ; that the writer of the Epistle to the Hebrews was concerned with a group whose general outlook was akin to that of Alexandrian Judaism ; and that the Fourth Evangelist was in touch with an even wider circle, which included some belonging to a purely Hellenistic background, " a wide public consisting primarily of devout and thoughtful persons (for the thoughtless and religiously indifferent would never trouble to open such a book as this) in the varied and cosmopolitan society of a great Hellenistic city such as Ephesus under the Roman Empire."[1]

All these groups shared, in greater or less degree, the images and language-forms to which I have referred for they were in free circulation among the varying cultural communities—Rabbinic, Philonic, Hermetic and perhaps Gnostic—to be found in the world of that time. So we find Paul freely using such symbolic terms as Image, Heavenly Man, Wisdom, Temple, Body, Logos, Son of God, the First Born of Creation, the New Creation. We find the writer of the Epistle to the Hebrews speaking of the Son, the Logos, the First Begotten, the Image, the High-Priest, Temple, Body, Sacrifice. And we find the Fourth Evangelist employing a rich vocabulary of current terms—Logos, Son, Temple, Body, Birth from above—together with such common symbolic forms as light, life, the way, the vine, the bread, the shepherd, as he sought to convey the Christian gospel to his mixed audience.

Moreover, we find in the writings of these evangelists a ready use of the general building *methods* which were employed in the cultural circles of their day. There is the *allegory*, so constantly used by Philo, occasionally appearing in the writings of St. Paul, and a major tool of the writer of the Epistle to the Hebrews. There is the *comparison*—sometimes a straightforward simile and sometimes an analogy— appearing in the Pauline writings (the body and its

[1] Dodd. Op. cit., 9.

members, the grafting process, the bridegroom and the bride) and still more often in the Johannine (the door, the lamb of God, the corn of wheat falling into the ground). There is the *type and antitype*, used by Paul sometimes in argument and sometimes in exhortation, used by the writer to the Hebrews as one of his most important literary devices.

Above all there is the *sign* of the Fourth Gospel. In his illuminating discussion of the use of symbolism in the Gospel, Professor Dodd points out that there are two main forms in which this symbolism appears. On the one hand there are the key-symbols such as the Shepherd, the Vine, the Bread, the Water, with their extended elaborations and applications : on the other hand there are the stories such as the turning of the water into wine, the healing of the blind man, and the raising of Lazarus, with their symbolic allusions. He compares this treatment of symbols with that of Plato and in part of Philo, and concludes that the evangelist had clear affinities with the contemporary philosophy which regarded the visible world as a copy of the world of invisible realities.[1] This means that every earthly vine bodies forth in some way the eternal idea of Vine, every shepherd the eternal idea of Shepherdhood, every visible light in this world the eternal idea of Light. It is therefore abundantly evident that the early Christian evangelists were quick to use images, language-forms, shapes, patterns, and building methods employed by the great religious myth-makers of their time.

[1] Op. cit. 139-40

But was this all ? Were they content simply to press the Christ and His Gospel into the moulds that were ready to their hand ? Clearly they were not. They succeeded in making a real translation, a magnificent transposition. But it involved one major, radical substitution at the very heart of things which, just because it was at the heart of things, affected literally everything. Where the Greek had looked at reality and interpreted the whole of reality through either the Logos or the Idea, where the Rabbinic Jew had looked at reality through the Torah, the Christian evangelist looked at and interpreted reality wholly through the Living Person, Jesus of Nazareth, the Word and Image of God. He it is who is at the centre of the myth of creation : He it is who upholds all things by the word of His power. The words, the images, the patterns may be familiar : but the central transforming Agent, though he may bear names and titles which are familiar, is new, is unfamiliar, is unique : He is none other than the Jesus who walked in Galilee and taught in Jerusalem, who suffered and died and rose again, Jesus the Saviour of the world.

Many illustrations could be given of the way in which these evangelists constantly start from and return to this central point of light which illuminates the whole. One of the most dramatic is the sudden proclamation of John 1, 14. It was many years later that one who had himself been steeped in the categories of Greek culture[1] confessed that whereas the words and ideas and method of development of the

[1] St. Augustine.

CHRISTIAN COMMUNICATION 73

first thirteen verses would have been entirely congenial to him as a Platonist, the 14th verse would
have been utterly unintelligible and unacceptable.
Probably he would never have been brought to make
such a confession had he not *seen* the continuing life
of this Jesus, the Word of God, being manifested in
the life-pattern of certain of his contemporaries.
Nevertheless, once the change at the centre of his
own system of reality had been made, it became
possible for the system itself to be used as a medium
for making a major impact upon the culture of his
day.

Even more significant in the matter of the " signs "
of the Fourth Gospel, is the constant witness of the
evangelist to the fact that the eternal shepherdhood
(e.g.) which according to the Platonic philosophy
belonged only to the invisible world, had actually
been manifested in the One Who acted in space and
time as a shepherd of men and laid down His life for
the sheep : the eternal light had actually come into
the world and given light to those who were in darkness : the eternal Bread had actually revealed Himself
as the bread-giver in an acted " sign " and thereby
revealed Himself as able to give his flesh for the life
of the world : the eternal life had actually been lifted
up upon a Cross of suffering and death so that He
might draw all men to Himself. He *is* the Life,
Light, Shepherd, Vine—all familiar symbols—but it
is actually in His incarnate life that these symbols
find their definitive expression and confirmation. The
whole universe, for this evangelist, revolves around

One Whose career has been *seen* and Whose significance has been *expressed* through words which make up the one supreme Logos of reality.

So far as the writer to the Hebrews is concerned, his altogether distinctive contribution to the process of transposition is his adoption of the imagery of the High-Priest in the sanctuary, with the subsequent identification of Jesus with the High-Priest and the offering of His body with the sacrifice. The setting is general but the central figure is unique : the patterns are recurring but His offering is once for all : the imagery is familiar but the One Who in the days of His flesh offered up strong crying and tears and learned obedience through the things that He suffered is without parallel in any other record.

Perhaps the most interesting feature of St. Paul's contribution is the fact that it was really made on two fronts. On the one hand he was steeped in the thought-patterns and highly trained in the methodology of Rabbinic Judaism : on the other hand he was familiar with certain aspects of Hellenism and as time went on had increasingly to come to grips with it. As far as the former was concerned, W. D. Davies makes it clear that St. Paul continued in many ways to move within the framework of the Rabbinic system. But again at the centre a radical substitution had taken place. The Second Adam is Jesus the Christ : the new Creation is in and through Jesus the Christ : the Wisdom of God, the Image of God, the Glory of God, is not the Torah but the same Jesus the Christ : the Body of the New Man, the Israel of the New

Creation, is the Church of Jesus the Christ. All things had become new as they were viewed, not through the Torah, but through the gospel of the Christ. And on the Hellenistic front the questions of how the universe had been created and how it was sustained allowed of only one answer. The Son of God, Jesus Christ, is " the image of the invisible God, the first-born of all creation ; for in Him all things were created . . . and for Him. He is before all things and in Him all things hold together."

All this leads us to conclude that in the first great adventure of translation and transposition that had to be made, the Christian evangelists availed themselves of that part of the Hebrew tradition which had already, in certain respects, been adjusted to the Hellenistic world and that in addition they made themselves familiar with the images and ideas and verbal symbols and language-patterns already in general circulation. They did not just translate certain formulæ into approximate verbal equivalents. They pierced to the heart of the other culture and there, at that central point, they set the living presence of Jesus the Christ, the Christ revealed through that Jesus Who had lived and suffered and died and risen again. From that centre they stretched out to embrace the whole universe of Hellenism. The Gospel, born in prophecy and history, had begun to be translated into the language of symbol and myth.

CHAPTER FIVE

The Story Continues

I. THE CENTRALITY OF CHRIST

THE EARLIEST formulation of the Christian Gospel
was expressed, I have suggested, in words and images
characteristic of a prophetic community living " between the times " (and between civilisations). Past
and future, despair and hope, bondage and freedom,
had come together in the " Now " : and the " Now "
was no mere empty moment—it marked the critical
change wrought by the saving work of Jesus Christ.
It is surely impossible to evade the sense of urgency
and exultancy which characterises the earliest Christian
kerygma.[1] What had been looked for has happened,
the longed-for salvation has arrived. The history of
God's elect has been gathered up and fulfilled in the
mighty achievement of Jesus the Christ. What this
meant for the future was hardly yet in question. Men
lived joyously in the new era which had been inaugurated by the great redemption.

It is not certain that even in the preaching of Jesus
Himself the prophetic and eschatological notes were

[1] *Kerygma*. A Greek term denoting the Gospel (i.e. the good news con-
cerning Jesus and His salvation) as preached or proclaimed rather than as
expressed in written form.

the only ones that were heard. Some of the parables suggest that He was not unmindful of forms of life, individual and social, which possess a more regular and settled pattern. Be that as it may, it is certain that the early evangelists, as soon as they began to use the Greek language to convey their proclamation, and as soon as they sought to show the relevance of their message within a Greek milieu, found that a radical transposition had to take place. Of that translation and transposition I have given some account in chapter four. The essential *kerygma* with its prophetic and eschatological notes was not lost : it breaks in again and again into every situation and into every communication of the New Testament. But the symbolic and the mythological had also to be evangelised and perhaps the greatest wonder of early Christianity is that the central place in each was claimed for Jesus the Christ. The New Testament ends with the Christ at the centre of the covenant community and of its history, at the centre of the Divine organism and of its myth. Potentially He is at the centre of every community and its history, of every social organism and its myth.

II.   THE GOSPEL IN THE MEDIÆVAL WORLD

The next important stage in the history of the communication of the Gospel was the translation of essential Christian truth into the Latin language. But this transposition presented no difficulties comparable to those which beset the first great adventure into the Greek world of thought. For the Roman genius never concerned itself with constructing a total world-view or with speculating about the nature of process and reality. Rather it was content to devote its energy to organising life according to well defined patterns and to constructing an imposing system of law capable of maintaining a high degree of social order. Thus it was ready, to a large extent, to take over whatever philosophy and science it needed from the Greeks and any theology which attracted its interest from the devotees of Oriental religions. Having taken over a philosophy or a theology, it was quite prepared to use its own tools—the Latin language, its legal forms, its ritual patterns—to apply it to individual and social life. In the process both the system of ideas and the tools themselves were bound to be affected in certain respects, but the change was more in the realm of organisation and formulation than in that of speculation and interpretation.

The Latin language was well qualified to give a clear translation of history and narrative, a precise formulation of doctrine and ethics and liturgy, and a ready-made vocabulary for the designation of grades and orders and functions within the social organisation of the Church. But it did not provide a terminology which was universal and timeless in its outreach : it did not approve of leaving avenues open for advance, for change, or for exciting adventures in ideas. It sharpened distinctions and made clear definitions, it gave Christianity a vocabulary for certain aspects of its life. But it had not the resources to become an adequate transmitter of the lively Hebraic-Hellenic dialectic which the Scriptures themselves contained and which the Christian faith, in its continuing life, displayed. The Roman temperament and the Latin language were already too set in their forms to become channels for the communication of the full dynamic of the Christian Gospel. They have made a distinctive contribution in the realms of law and liturgy but on the whole have tended to press the Christian revelation into their own static moulds rather than allow the immense vitality of the new faith to regenerate both language and life.

The Eastern Churches, though possessing in the Greek language a medium which was more flexible and more easily applicable to eternal realities than the Latin, became largely content to remain within the circle of their own rhythms and regularities of doctrine and liturgy and to lose sight of the eschatological implications of their Hebraic heritage. Indeed, as time went on they often seemed unconscious of any continuing responsibility to inquire into the nature and meaning of their environment in the way which had been characteristic of their Greek forefathers. It was not until the Middle Ages, with the gradual recovery of the Greek inheritance through the Renaissance and the more sudden recovery of the Hebraic inheritance through the Reformation that new media became available by which the full Christian Gospel could be communicated in more adequate and effective ways.

Through the whole movement of the Renaissance

it was not only the Greek language and notable works
of Greek literature that were re-discovered : it was
also the richly variegated world of the classical age
with its authentic images and essential forms. Men
began to see again through the eyes of the Greeks
and to look at the universe in the way the Greeks
had done. They began to be intensely interested, not
only in the inhabitants and the structures of the
heavenly world, but also in those of the world by
which they were themselves surrounded. In other
words, the way began to open up for the Christian
faith which had sprung to life in the world of first-
century Hellenism and had at that time vigorously
related itself to the images and language-forms of its
day, to be related to the actual world in which men
were living in the thirteenth, fourteenth and fifteenth
centuries and to cease to be regarded as a purely
other-worldly affair. The renewal of life and language
in Italy, Spain, France and the Low Countries was in
no small measure due to this epoch-making change.

This, however, was not the only ferment at work
in Europe. The frontier nations on the northern and
eastern boundaries of the old Roman Empire were
growing in confidence and in a new desire for self-
determination. They had begun to grow conscious of
their apparently inferior status and of their dependence upon the more civilised lands to the south
and west for their cultural inspiration. But the new
stirrings of interest in the language and literature of
the past were soon to lead to a revival of Biblical
studies and to an earnest desire to have the Bible

available in the common languages of the peoples of the north. To be confronted by the world of the Bible, however, proved to be an even more startling and revolutionary experience than that of being allowed access into the world of the classical age.

Here was the vivid story of a people, the Hebrews, whose historical situations and experiences often seemed astonishingly similar to those of the subject peoples of northern Europe. The Hebrews had struggled for their liberty and for the right to pursue their God-given destiny, and in the struggle God had acted for them, visiting and redeeming His people. The images and language-forms of the salvation-history of the Bible were exactly applicable to the situation in history which was the lot of those nations and communities which were ultimately to be called " Protestant." " Elect," " faith," " covenant," " justification," " redemption," " kingdom," and a host of other terms gained an altogether new vitality and meaning in the circumstances of the Reformation age. It seemed to the new nations as if Abraham and Isaac and Jacob were their own forefathers : as if the prophets were the precursors of their own fight for liberty and self-determination : as if in Christ their own history had been reconstituted and as if they were living over again the New Testament experience of the great emancipation.

Thus the stories and oracles and parables of the Bible found a strangely congenial medium in the languages of the peoples who were struggling out of their position of tutelage and subordination into a

new sense of self-confidence and destiny. Yet the
language had already assimilated a good deal of the
classical heritage through the influence of the Western
Church and through the advance of the new learning
across Europe. So it came about that the vernaculars
served as the vehicle for the communication both
of the Biblical salvation-history and its attendant
language-forms on one side of the classical myth and
its appropriate images on the other side. In English,
the Bible on the one side, Shakespeare and Milton on
the other ; in German, Luther's Bible on the one
hand, Schiller and Goethe on the other. And in the
process of this dual communication the languages
themselves expanded and increased their powers, and
to no small extent these new language-forms made
possible the great advances of Western culture in the
next four centuries.

III.   THE GOSPEL IN THE MODERN WORLD

Soon the peoples of the West were to encounter
tribes and languages of whose existence they had
hitherto been entirely ignorant. In the New World,
in Africa and the East, the trader and the adventurer,
followed by the coloniser and the missionary, began
to break through the barriers which separated the
settled civilisations of the East and the tribal cultures
of primitive peoples from the dynamic and outward-
looking nations of Europe. In this enterprise, the
first serious attempt to bridge the gulf of language
was made by Protestant missionaries who were fired

by the determination to make the Scriptures available in every native tongue. As the result of almost incredible patience and unceasing labour, one language after another was made the vehicle of the Biblical revelation, though only very gradually were the other treasures of Western culture expressed in these new forms. And in point of fact the world-view which had been originally taken over into Christianity from the Græco-Roman world and transformed by the setting of the figure of the Christ at the centre, hardly had the chance to make any determinative impression upon the non-European cultures of the world before another view of the universe began[1] to make its appearance and ultimately to assume an almost complete control of the Western imagination.

The rise of modern science has provided a myth of the universe more comprehensive in its inclusiveness and more extensive in its appeal than any of the earlier formulations of the great cultures of mankind. The great myths of the Egyptian, the Indian, the Chinese and the Hellenistic cultures, were all considerably influenced by *local* conditions and circumstances. The views of nature and the heavens, the cycle of the seasons and the rhythm of the life-process, were derived from patient observation of and reflection

[1] It is true that Roman Catholic missions sought to take over many of the images and symbolic forms from paganism and to integrate them into the Christian myth. Their policy was not to destroy but to bring to a true fulfilment. Rightly handled, this could mean that the figure of the Christ was set at the centre of the culture that was being evangelised. All too often, however, it meant that the Christ and Christian symbols were allowed a place within a very mixed company of pagan deities and their symbolic representations.

What else is "?!
" Catholic Theology

upon the data supplied by a relatively limited environment. It is true that travellers and traders went far
afield and brought back reports of what they had
seen. But the over-all framework of the cultural myth
was still provided by the stabilities and regularities of
the *local* situation. The myth was in a sense the great
projection into the beyond of what had been observed
within the boundaries of the existence of a delimited
cultural group.

But now in the seventeenth century a situation had
arisen in which man had circumnavigated the globe
and had, through the telescope, gained new knowledge
of the motions of the heavenly bodies. For the first
time it had become possible to construct a framework
which would, it was increasingly assumed, include
the *whole* universe. The laws of this universe were
to become increasingly known : the rhythms and
regularities of nature were to become increasingly
plain : the origins and sustaining energies of the
life-process were to become increasingly open to
description and calculation. This myth would be
the transparent sphere through which *all* men might
view the whole universe for although there might be
peculiarities of local circumstance and details of
unexplored areas waiting to be integrated into the
picture, nature as a whole was the same for *all* people
and its myth was therefore of universal application.

Moreover, as the construction of the great myth of
modern science proceeded, it became increasingly
difficult to imagine a *beyond*, either in space or time.
Man's universe could be conceived as a vast spatial

sphere within which earth, sun and innumerable stars constantly turned and wheeled, but any beyond in space seemed infinitely remote : the time-span could be conceived as beginning millions of years ago and stretching on into millions of years ahead, but again the " beyond " in time seemed infinitely far away. In other words, the comparatively rapid transposition of the scientific myth into the world's imagination meant that more and more were adopting a world-view in which all meaningful existence was enclosed within a vast mechanical system whose laws could be learned and whose processes could be harnessed to the supply of man's material needs.[1]

The early efforts of pioneering missionaries to translate and transpose Christian truth into other languages had been magnificent but these efforts had scarcely been launched when the flood-waters of technological progress, interpreted and sustained by the scientific myth, began to roll around the world and submerge the imagination of the peoples of mankind. Before the meagre resources of Christian missions had scarcely begun to set the Christ, the Word of God, at the centre of the world's myths, the vast resources of modern technology were bringing the mighty machine, the symbolic representation of the scientific myth, into the very heart of the life and outlook of one people after another. The task of the Christian missionary was thus magnified a thousand-

[1] Paul Tillich affirms that the characteristic concept of the twentieth century is that of the " technical reason " being used to perfect the " technical society."

fold. Not only must he seek to replace the myths of Brahman and Tao and a hundred less imposing formulations : he must also seek to save men from being captivated by the myth of the soulless machine.

But the growth of the scientific myth has not been the only major development of modern times which has complicated the work of the missionary and made his task of translation increasingly difficult. The other complicating factor has been concerned with the interpretation of history. As I have already suggested, much of the appeal of the Scriptures at the time of the Reformation was due to the fact that the historical situations portrayed in the sacred record had a definite kinship with the precise situations of the newly self-conscious nations into whose languages they were being translated. The approach to a universal historical redemption through the experiences of a particular people whose history was recorded in the Bible, made sense and created meaning for peoples who were passing through similar experiences themselves. It was not too hard to transpose the story of freedom achieved and destiny promised into the languages of peoples who were struggling for freedom and searching for destiny.

Scarcely any of the peoples to whom the modern missionary movement came, however, were in this position. Some were conscious of the sinister and threatening powers of evil spirits and demonic forces : there were Biblical situations parallel to these but they were in the general realm of myth rather than of history. Some were conscious of the inferiorities and frustrations which were theirs by reason of distinctions of caste, class or possessions : there were Biblical situations parallel to these but freedom was conceived largely in other-worldly terms rather than as involving radical changes and new destinies within this world. It was only gradually during the nineteenth century that stirrings of a wider sense of national destiny began to appear, and only in the twentieth century that the great awakening of all the peoples of the world began to take place.

Some of these stirrings had undoubtedly been stimulated by the story of the struggle for freedom enshrined in the Biblical literature and translated into the experience of the peoples of northern Europe in the sixteenth and seventeenth centuries. But the great awakening came rather as a result of the spectacle of the internecine wars of the West, as an outcome of the Eastern nations' growing consciousness of their own material resources, and as a consequence of the dramatic change which had come to the world through the Russian revolution. Suddenly the peoples awoke to the fact that the West was not invincible. They, too, had destinies to fulfil and the only way by which they could be fulfilled was by throwing off the yoke of the domination of the West. They talked of freedom, they looked forward to the hour of destiny : they were ready to give their allegiance to Messianic deliverers : they began to realise that history was meaningful and the time-category real. Here perhaps was the new situation which would provide the basic categories for translating the

Biblical story of redemption and destiny into the authentic language-forms of all the peoples of the world.

But alas ! this bright prospect has been dimmed by two most serious obstructing factors. On the one hand Christianity, in the minds of the peoples of the world, was essentially the religion of the nations of the West : how was it possible to be free from the domination of the West if the religion of the West was retained ? On the other hand, and even more serious, a rival interpretation of history had appeared, derived ultimately from the same cultural milieu as Christianity,[1] but finding the meaning of universal history in the emergence of a classless society whose members would all share alike in the earth's material resources. What better hope was there of attaining economic freedom than by accepting the gospel of Marxism and by becoming intègrated into the communist society ?

Thus at the very time when the world's languages have begun to react to the challenges of new situations and new prospects and thereby to provide terms and categories more akin to those needed by the Christian gospel of crisis and redemption, of oppression and deliverance—at that very time the Christian Gospel has come under deep suspicion because of its association in history with the imperialistic powers of the West and because of its apparent indifference to the great struggle for economic equality which is going on in virtually every country of the world. Language-

[1] Karl Marx's parents were orthodox Jews.

forms are becoming available, but the mighty task of setting the full redemption which is in Christ Jesus at the centre of history, rather than either the political emancipation of a particular society or the economic emancipation of the universal society, has scarcely begun to be accomplished.

Only when His redemption of society in *all* its aspects (not simply the political or the economic) comes to be recognised as the centre of human history and His justification of the *whole* man (not simply man in his sense of political inferiority or economic inequality) as the symbol of human destiny, only then will the real work of transposition be effectively achieved. Yet with nothing less can the Christian translator be satisfied.

CHAPTER SIX

What is the Essential Message?

LET US now turn back to the four questions listed at the end of chapter one. In this chapter I shall seek to define the essential message more clearly in the light of our inquiry about word and image : in the next chapter I shall try to indicate what are some of the essential qualifications of the one who aspires to communicate the essential message. In the final chapters I shall consider the other two questions—those of the techniques and language-forms appropriate for the transmission of this particular message.

1. JESUS AS THE LORD OF HISTORY

So far as the essential message is concerned it has already become clear that the severely simple expression of the message in such a verbal form as " Christ Jesus came into the world to save sinners " or in such a visual form as the crucifix (even when it is the victorious Christ who is regnant on the tree) is not in itself enough. Some historical interpretation of the terms " Christ " and " Jesus " must be provided, some historical context of the cross-resurrection complex must be supplied, if such a word or such an image is to penetrate meaningfully into any situation. On the other hand the comprehensive totality of verbal forms provided by the canonical Scriptures cannot be regarded as constituting the *essential* Christian message : nor can the message be held to be necessarily expressed through the vast comprehensive totality of visual patterns supplied by the institutions and ritual-forms of a historical Catholic Church.

If then neither the severely simple nor the highly complex is to be regarded as the essential communication, in what direction shall we look for more adequate criteria of formulation? I suggest that the main conclusion to which our inquiry so far has pointed is that there must be a *history* of Jesus the Christ, there must also be a *myth* of Christ the Son of God, but that in neither case shall we ever be able to claim that the definitive form either of the history or of the myth has been finally attained. Moreover, neither the history nor the myth is sufficient of itself to constitute the essential gospel. Both are necessary and whereas the one possesses the capacity of making a special appeal to the ear, the primary appeal of the other is to the eye. In relation to particular cultures and at particular periods of history one or the other will seem to gain the ascendancy. But it is through the living interaction of the two and not through the exclusive sovereignty of the one that the essential Christian gospel can be continuously proclaimed.

In the New Testament the activity of Jesus of

Nazareth is declared to have been the actual fulfilment of the history of the Jewish people and the
potential fulfilment of the history of every people. In
the forefront stands the proclamation that the
dominant categories which had come to express the
historical expectation of the Jews—the Kingdom, the
Redemption, the Messiah, the Son of Man, the End
and the New Beginning—had actually gained their
realisation and their fulfilment through the achievements of Jesus of Nazareth. There is no evidence
that in the earliest preaching stress was laid upon the
ethical teaching or even upon the parables of Jesus.
The whole stress was upon what Jesus had done :
His works of mercy, His miracles of healing, His
submission to death and His victory over death, His
pouring out of the Holy Spirit of the new age. What
He had done constituted the true fulfilment of Old
Testament expectation and it was therefore possible
to acclaim Him as the Christ, the true Servant of God.

This message was related to Israel's historical
experience and declared the fulfilment of that experience but it could not be expressed in any final
way in terms of that experience alone. The terms
Kingdom, Messiah, Redemption, were wonderfully
appealing but they were not in themselves finally
determinative. The Kingdom which Jesus inaugurated transcended any conception of Kingdom
hitherto entertained : the Messiahship of Jesus transcended any Messianic expectation which had been
formulated in Israel's historical experience. In particular, the Jewish expectation had never ceased to be

this-worldly in its central conception of the locus of the rule of God nor had it ceased to be moralistic in its ultimate view of the nature of the rule of God. Through the work of Jesus it was declared once and for all that the perfect rule of God is only realisable in a realm beyond space and time and only operative in an area of relationships which transcends law and tradition. Through the redemption wrought by Christ men had been delivered out of the power of darkness and translated into the kingdom of the Son of God's love : they had been rescued from the slavery of law and admitted into the glorious liberty of the children of God. In other words, Israel's historical expectation had been fulfilled but in the moment of fulfilment it had been transcended and transformed.

Such a fulfilment and transformation can never be finally expressed by means of a single historical formulation. Continuing research into the nature of the event-patterns and language-forms of Israel's history enables us to gain a clearer view of the process of which Jesus' work was the fulfilment. But that research cannot be carried on in isolation from the histories of other nations and the expectations of other peoples. In fact, the history of every people casts some light on Israel's history and vice versa. This means that fuller knowledge of the world's history can enable us to gain a clearer understanding of the forms and categories employed to recount the story of Israel's history : at the same time the crucial story, which is declared to be the fulfilment and transforma-

tion of Israel's history, can be seen as the true fulfilment and transformation of every people's history—
as indeed the centre and fulfilment of *all* history. The
story of the saving acts of Jesus, the acts by which
He was declared to be the Saviour and Lord of the
whole historical process—this is one part of the
essential message of the Christian Gospel.

II. JESUS AS THE WORD OF INTERPRETATION

But it is also true that in the New Testament the
person of the incarnate Son of God is declared to
have been the actual centre of the mythological world-
picture of that era and the symbolical centre of the
world-picture of any era. In the later writings of the
New Testament there is the clear affirmation that the
categories which were being used in the mythology
of that time—Eternal Life, the Logos, Heaven and
Earth, the High-Priest of Creation—had gained their
centre of illumination and concentration of meaning
in and through Jesus, the Son of God. Again the
stress is not laid at first upon the moral qualities or
the æsthetic excellencies revealed in the daily life of
the incarnate Son. Instead the concentration of
interest is upon the way in which Jesus supplies in
His own person the confirmation of the speculations
and the answer to the deepest questionings of His
own particular age.

What, for example, men asked, was the secret of
eternal life? Was it to be found in withdrawing from
the things of the body into the pure realm of spirit?

Was it to be discovered in and through the contemplation of ideal forms or through the vision of ideal beauty ? Or wherein was the ultimate meaning of the universe to be found ? Was it expressible through some logical structure which could gather into a simple form the laws and sequences of the observable universe ? Or how was heaven connected with earth ? Was there some way by which heavenly spirits could incarnate themselves in earthly forms or by which creatures of earth could ascend to heaven ? How had the visible world in space and time come into existence and how could it return to its true home in the realm of invisible timeless reality ?

Such were the questions which the mythologies of the Mediterranean world of the first century were framed to answer. They might vary in details but they shared the same over-all pattern or framework. The universe was regarded as two-storeyed. Heaven, the realm of pure form and rhythmic movement, of pure spirit and eternal life, stood over and above earth, the realm of distortion and disorder, of the material and the transient. How could there be connections and associations between the one and the other ? If there was a Logos, how could that Logos be known ? If there was a pathway from earth to heaven, how could that pathway be found ?

These were the mythological categories within which the essential Christian message had to be expressed. And the earliest Christian witnesses were bold enough to take them and use them as they bore witness to the essential nature of the Son of God. He

is the Logos, they said : in Him is eternal life. He
brings heaven to earth, He lifts earth to heaven. He
is the High-Priest of the whole created order : He is
the Source from which all things take their origin.
Yet as in the case of the historical formulation, there
was no finality of expression in this mythological
formulation. Logos, Image of the Invisible God,
The Mediator descending from heaven to earth and
ascending from earth to heaven, were wonderfully
expressive but they were not in themselves all-
embracing. The Logos actually assuming human
flesh, the Image gloriously unveiled in a human life,
the descent and ascent dramatised within the gamut
of a human experience, eternal life realised within a
Divine-human relationship—these were more than
expressions of already existing categories, they were
transfigurations. In other words, the myth of the
Mediterranean world was radically changed as a
personal career was acknowledged as the way, the
meaning, the life of the whole.

Continuing research into the nature of the world-
structures and language-forms of the Hellenistic age
enables us to gain a clearer view of the myth of which
Jesus' career became the centre and the meaning.
But that myth must be modified both in form and
expression in the light of fuller knowledge of the
universe. Not that it is likely to be entirely out-
moded by subsequent discovery though the coming
of the modern scientific age has necessitated greater
revolutions in the world's mythology than ever
before. Still, however, man is seeking to obtain a

total picture of his universe, still he is seeking to formulate its rhythms and regularities, still he is seeking to find a way from the disordered and transient to the harmonious and abiding. And still the essential message of the Christian Gospel is that through the incarnation of the Son of God the answer has been given to all these questions though never precisely in their own terms. For the life-pattern of the Son of God cannot be expressed as a law or a principle or a formula or an equation. It is a life-pattern of *personal* involvement and *personal* redemption, of incarnation and transfiguration, of death and life, of *kenosis* and *plerosis*. This pattern of humiliation and glorification through death and resurrection constituting the central meaning of every mythology—here is the other part of the essential message of the Christian Gospel.

III.   A STORY AND A PICTURE

My conclusion, then, is that the essential Christian message consists of a story and a picture. The *story* tells of the activities of Jesus of Nazareth : it reaches its climax in the record of His suffering, death and resurrection-appearances. And Christian witnesses have declared and still declare that in this story all history finds the key to its significance and the pointer to its goal. The meaning of history, it is claimed, is to be found not in the attainment of political independence nor in the achievement of economic self-sufficiency nor in the acquiring of class dominance.

The goal of history is to be found not in the possession by all men of material comforts and physical well-being nor in the elimination of all inequalities of status and class. Rather, so the Christian message proclaims, the meaning of history is to be found in the redemption of man from his earth-boundedness and self-centredness, the goal of history is to be found in the establishment of the perfect rule of God amongst men. All this has been made possible by the act of the Christ Who submitted Himself to the death which negates all material and selfish interests and rose again into the life of perfect enjoyment of the gracious rule of God. Something *happened* in history and the story of it must be told: hence the appeal to the word and to the ear. The story, too, must constantly be re-interpreted and re-applied to other histories, and in this way its significance will expand and grow. But the essential events of the Gospel-story stand firm in history and no message can ultimately call itself the *Christian* message which is not constantly returning to and wrestling with and being judged by and being renewed by the story of the saving acts of Jesus the Christ.[1]

The *picture* portrays a central figure whose personal career infolds itself around one burning centre—the place of death and resurrection—from which the whole is viewed and interpreted. Again Christian witnesses have sought to set this vision before the eyes of men under the conviction that in it and

[1] It is a striking fact that the story of the Cross plays a determinative part in the interpretations of history which appear in the writings of Arnold Toynbee and Reinhold Niebuhr and Herbert Butterfield.

through it the whole universe finds the secret of its own interpretation and the means of its own integration. The universe is to be interpreted, it is claimed, not as a random conglomeration of elements nor as a strictly predetermined evolutionary process nor as the continuing dialectic of two eternally opposing principles. The model for the integration of the universe is to be found not in a mystical formula nor in an impersonal rational principle nor in a machine nor even in some kind of servo-mechanism. Rather, so the Christian message implies, the universe is to be interpreted in terms of *personal* values, the model for its integration is to be found in a *personal* career. The meaning of the universe became incarnate and we beheld His glory—the outshining of grace and truth, the revelation of perfect sonship, the final unveiling of perfect sacrifice. The model of the universe was disclosed as a personal movement of self-fulfilment through self-identification, of the enrichment of spirit through involvement in matter, of the increase of energy through patient submission to forms of organisation.

By the incorporation of the Son of God within the organism of the created order the true meaning of the universe has been disclosed once for all. The appeal is primarily to the eye though only gradually was the Christian Church able to express the revelation through actual visual images—the earliest medium was the word-picture. But when, as in the period of the Middle Ages, art and philosophy combined to set the Christ at the very centre of the world-picture

" He (the Christ) pulled Western men from the depths of a moral and social confusion and despair perhaps greater than, but not totally unlike, that of the contemporary world ; having His referential roots initially in the Greek science and philosophy of Plato, as it was mediated and developed theologically through Plotienus and St. Augustine, He integrated man's empirical knowledge, his emotional and religious intuitions, and the highest and most sober reflections of his intellect into one meaningful and triumphant whole." (F. S. C. Northrop. *The Meeting of East and West*. 285.)

Such an integration could not be final in form seeing that man is ever gaining new knowledge of his universe and its continuing life. But with every new disclosure man needs to return in imagination to the picture of the incarnation of the Son of God which the New Testament portrays. Only in the light of that picture can a truly *Christian* interpretation of the universe be constructed in any age. Only when the personal Christ with His revelation of personal values and personal ends is set at the centre of the world-picture of any period can a truly *Christian* integration of life be achieved.

CHAPTER SEVEN

The Missionary Character

I. THE MISSIONARY AND HIS HISTORY

FROM THE communication let us turn to the communicator. What are the essential characteristics of the missionary in every age? Here again no final answers can be given. Perhaps the nearest approach to a direct answer is to say that the communicator must himself be ever engaged in the struggle to distinguish between a too light and a too heavy equipment for his task. He may, with great heroism, determine to leave virtually everything behind him. He abandons Western ways and customs, he learns a new language and pattern of life, he proclaims the simple gospel of salvation and no more. But although he may have some initial success, it gradually becomes clear that the Gospel needs to be related to a man's whole social and natural environment as well as to the needs of his individual soul ; indeed the needs of the soul cannot really be diagnosed or expressed apart from some reference to the wider context within which the individual lives. If, then, the Christian message is to be effectively proclaimed something more is needed than can be conveyed by the isolated individual addressing himself to the isolated soul.

But is the solution then to be found in a determination to transplant the whole complex of social organisation, ritual practices and doctrinal formularies belonging to a Western Christian denomination into the soil of an Eastern or African environment? Again, there may be some initial success if the resources in man-power and money are sufficient to build up a relatively imposing model of traditional church life in non-Christian surroundings. But such a structure will inevitably be weak and impermanent unless the attempt is being constantly made to relate the old forms to the new environments, allowing much of the old to die in order that a new and truly indigenous life may be made manifest.

A fuller answer to the question of essential qualifications may be framed by retaining the division between history and myth which I made when considering the essential Christian message. If it is true that the story of the saving acts of Jesus the Christ stands for all time as the key to the meaning and goal of history, then it is essential that anyone who aspires to be a communicator of the Christian message shall have found the central reference point of his own personal history in the same story of Jesus Christ and His Cross. For no one can contract out of his own history. He has a past and that past cannot be undone.

The Moving Finger writes ; and having writ,
Moves on : not all your Piety nor Wit
   Shall lure it back to cancel half a Line,
Nor all your Tears wash out a Word of it. . . .

This is true. And it means that a man's past is bound
to go with him wherever he journeys in life. But
although the past has been written and cannot be
cancelled, the *interpretation* of what has been written
has by no means been settled and determined in the
same inexorable way. It may, for example, be interpreted in terms of privilege to be held on to at all
costs. The privilege of nationality, of family, of
education—all may be regarded as having conferred
an indelible status which is in some way superior to
that of any other class. Or personal history may be
interpreted in terms of misfortune : the handicap of
ill-health or of an unsettled home or of an indifferent
education may be regarded as having produced
disabilities and distortions such as can never be
overcome.

That a man is supported by some aspects of his
past and handicapped by others it would be foolish
to deny. For the winning of a position in society,
for the attainment of success in business, for the
acquiring of a skill in arts and crafts, all of these
factors are important. But that they are finally
determinative for the task of communicating the
Christian Gospel I should strenuously deny. Neither
successes nor failures, neither privileges nor mis-
fortunes, in themselves determine the future. He

who embraces the Christian message affirms that the
judging-saving work of Jesus the Christ which
found critical expression in His Cross and Resurrection, redeems his own past from all pride of privilege,
from all resentment of misfortune, and sends him
forward into the future with this same standard of
judgment to be applied to every aspect of his subsequent historical experience.

No more vivid illustration could be found of the
man who has made the story of the saving work of
Christ the centre and touchstone of his own personal
history than that which is provided by the auto-
biographical fragment in Philippians 3. Here was a
man who possessed all the marks of privilege within
a particular historical tradition. His pedigree, his
tribal status, his religious dedication, his formal
education, his personal commitment, had been such
that by every standard of Jewish orthodoxy and by
every sanction of national tradition he was justified
in regarding himself as successful, superior, and secure.
He was surely in a position, if ever a man was, to
communicate religious truth to the ignorant and
under-privileged. Yet he had submitted every part
of his historical inheritance to the judgment of the
Cross. Nothing could be removed but everything
could be re-interpreted. Those things which had
seemed positive gain could be judged as of no account
in the service of Christ: those things which had
seemed to be hindrances and handicaps might well
prove positive assets in the new order of living. In
any case there was henceforth to be no final con-

fidence in the heritage from personal past history. "Forgetting those things which are behind and reaching forth unto those things which are before" —this was the "character" of the missionary to the Gentiles whose whole historical existence was constantly being re-submitted to the criterion revealed in the history of Jesus the. Christ.

The missionary to-day cannot escape from his own history, national, social or individual. But it is his duty, as far as possible, to become *aware* of that history and to bring it under the judgment of the central touchstone of history. Only so can he dare to approach those who belong to a different historical tradition and whose personal histories are very different from his own. He will become aware of their own pride of history, their own aspirations for a richer historical destiny. He will judge these not solely in the context of his own historical framework but in the light of that history held under the judgment of the Cross and the promise of the resurrection. It goes without saying that this is no easy task.[1] To wrestle with three histories simultaneously —my own history within its social context, my brother's history within its social context and the history of Jesus the Saviour of mankind within its social context—and then to relate these histories to one another in such a way that a meaningful redemption and a relevant hope begin to be formed : here is a task hard enough to tax the resources of the

[1] It is no easier for the man who has grown up in a tradition which is dominantly bourgeois and middle-class when he seeks relationship with one whose background is that of the factory and the trade union.

strongest. Yet nothing less is involved in a comprehensive communication of the Gospel of Jesus Christ.

II. THE MISSIONARY AND HIS WORLD

In the second place, if it be true that the picture of Jesus, the incarnate Son of God, stands for all time as the means of a comprehensive interpretation and integration of the universe, then it is essential that the one who seeks to be a communicator of that vision shall have found the focusing lens through which he views the whole of reality, in the same picture of eternal life revealed in Him. For no man can avoid coming to terms with the world in which he lives and moves and has his being. Myriads of images flash upon his vision in the course of a lifetime and without some integrative patterns life would be anarchic and even intolerable. But there are rhythms and regularities of inward experience, there are recurrences and reliabilities in the external world, and it is these which, in conjunction with images already present in the structure of the subconscious, gradually form themselves into a tolerably satisfying framework of existence. The succession of days and seasons can be expected to recur; the growth of the crops and the coming of the rain; the development of the human body, and the maturing of its potentialities; the variations of the sexes, and the processes of reproduction: all these gradually build themselves into a habitation of the imagination in which man can feel confident and secure.

But there is still the question of what it all means and whether it is really as secure as it seems. Often there come shocks when some part of the framework which had seemed utterly reliable suddenly disintegrates. Or there come revolutions in society when the whole of the accepted framework is threatened and the individual finds no stability in the existing order of things. And even when no such immediate shocks have to be faced the individual is never exempt from the necessity of asking ultimate questions about his universe. How can it be integrated? What does it all mean?

Is there one ultimate soul-substance which permeates and interpenetrates every part of the universe and is all life to be viewed in terms of a proper handling of this mysterious *mana*? Is there one ultimate world-soul behind all outward phenomena and is all existence to be viewed in terms of an entrance into an ever-deepening union with that mysterious Brahman? Is there one ultimate rational principle which controls and unifies the world and is human life to be viewed in terms of an increasing conformity to this mysterious *Logos*? Is there one ultimate evolutionary life-force which drives the world forward and is the wholeness of man's individual and social life to be viewed in terms of a growth in sensitivity of adaptation to this *élan vital*?

Or are there perhaps *two* ultimate principles struggling in the universe, light and darkness, spirit and matter, form and chaos, order and freedom, thesis and antithesis, man and nature, and is the whole of life to be viewed in terms of a proper resolution of this conflict? Are the two principles to be held in precarious balance or is the true meaning of life to be found in the firm control of one of the principles by the other? And is the content of the famous though ambiguous phrase, "man's standard of living," to be determined by his ultimate position of mastery within one or other of these conflicting pairs?

That men have found in and through these various world-views strength for living and answers to their questioning is obvious. For long periods such views have given a sense of wholeness and a vision of ordered meaning which have been deeply satisfying to the human imagination. And no man can fail to be profoundly influenced by the particular mythical framework which belongs to the society within which his own lot is cast. In considerable measure it determines the very way in which he the *sees* succession of fleeting images which passes before his eyes for the artifacts of any age are more and more determined in their *form* by the scientific world-view of the age to which they belong. Thus a machine or a dynamo proves to be not only the characteristic product of a particular age but also the model through which the viewing eye sees the universe in that age in an integrated and meaningful way.

All this means that the communicator's task is the supremely difficult one of holding together in some kind of creative relationship his own world-view, which he has almost unconsciously imbibed from the environment in which he has grown up, his brother's world-view gained in the same way and the Christian world-view if such there be. As I have already suggested, this task is from one point of view in process of becoming easier seeing that my own world-view is approximating more and more to my brother's world-view, in whatever environment he lives, because of the rapid spread of modern scientific knowledge and technique. It seems that the day can hardly be far distant when the whole world will be bound together within one generally accepted scientific world-view, however precisely this may be conceived and whatever pockets of resistance to such a view may still remain. From one angle this may simplify the missionary's task, though from another it will mean that the strength of what will then be a universally accepted framework will be all the greater as it stands over against the distinctively Christian world-view within which the missionary himself finds integration and meaning.

III.   THE CHRISTIAN MYTH

How, then, is it possible for the communicator to hold fast to an avowedly *Christian* myth when the scientific myth seems to be so firmly grounded and so near to universal acceptance? In chapter one I referred to Bultmann's solution which is, in effect, that the Christian myth deals with the ultimate problems of human existence—life and death, sin and redemption—and is therefore *independent* of the world-picture of any particular age. If this be so it means that the missionary's task is simplified for he can then proclaim his existential gospel within *any* environment, untroubled by the world-view which may form the framework of vision of those who live within it. That this has been done again and again in history and that it is being done to-day in many quarters is undoubtedly true. But that it is the true policy for those who are committed to a specifically *Christian* world-view or that it is even possible to deal with the problems of existence apart from the problems of environment is, I think, seriously open to question.

For it is of the essence of the *Christian* world-view that all things were created *in* the Son of God and *through* Him and *for* Him (John 1, 3., Col. 1, 16): through Him all things are sustained and in Him all things hold together; in the end all things will be subject to Him. This does not mean that all scientific inquiry and theoretical formulations are worthless. Nor does it mean that it is illegitimate to construct models to enable the human imagination to gain a clearer conception of the human environment. But it does mean that the ultimate structure of the universe is the expression of *personal* creativeness, that the sustaining energy of the universe is provided by *personal* self-outpouring, and that the goal of the universe is *personal* self-fulfilment. In other words, from beginning to end and at every stage of its existence the universe is to be interpreted in terms of the achievement of *personal* values and the attainment of *personal* ends. And the highly dramatic picture

which symbolises the whole process and every part
of the process is given in such a form as is provided
by the marvellous poem of Philippians 2.

> Who, being in the form of God
> thought it not robbery
> to be equal with God ;
> but made himself of no reputation,
> taking upon him the form of a servant,
> and being made in the likeness of men ;
> and being found in fashion as a man,
>   he humbled himself
> and became obedient unto death,
>   even the death of a cross.
> Wherefore God also hath highly exalted him
>   and given him a name
>   which is above every name ;
> that at the name of Jesus
>   every knee should bow,
> of things in heaven, and things
> in earth, and things under the earth
> and that every tongue should confess
>   that Jesus Christ is Lord,
> to the glory of God the Father.

The Christian missionary stands within this framework and through its windows he looks out upon the
universal scene. He sees every act of creation as the
taking form of that which has been conceived by the
personal imagination ; he sees the actual process as
involving a *personal* self-identification, a *personal*
ingression into the stuff out of which the finished

product is to be made, a *personal* humiliation through descent and disintegration and death ; he sees the fulfilment as the emergence of *personal* value, *personal* form, *personal* dominion. No haphazard interpretation of reality will do. No impersonal interpretation will suffice. The image through which all else is viewed is that which St. Paul describes as " the face of Jesus Christ." This is " the essential image which provides the light in which things must be studied and the form in which they can be understood " (John A. Mackay. *God's Order.* 2).

> That one Face, far from vanish, rather grows
> Become my universe that sees and knows.

In the last resort this aspect of the communicator's " character " cannot be described ; it can only be experienced. To see the image which provides the interpretation and the integration for the whole of existence is an experience which can only be portrayed obliquely by the aid of other images. For example, Mr. R. C. Hutchinson, writing of the novelist's impulse to create his work of art, describes it thus : " Suppose you are in Paris, travelling on the Metro. Standing near you there is a very old and very dirty woman. Beside her there is a tiny white-faced boy with spindle legs and a dribbly nose. The train lurches violently, and the old woman puts her hand on the boy's shoulder to steady him. He looks up at her, perhaps with a slight impatience, because he thinks he is too old for that sort of mothering. She looks down at him and smiles faintly. Then he smiles

back. You know, at once, that he is her grandson—
possibly her only grandchild. You know, at the same
moment, that all her love, all her pride, are centred
in him. But much more than that. In the instant
when those two people exchange that smile you see
represented a huge tract of human experience—*you
feel, all at once, that in the excitement and the beauty of
that exchange, everything in earth and heaven has been
revealed to you.*" (*The Listener.* April 2, 1953. 568.
Italics mine.)

Here is a controlling image giving meaning and
integration to man's total environment. The novelist's
testimony is impressive. Still more impressive, however, is the testimony of a great missionary who has
told, in a moving passage, how in actual fact, through
the pages of a letter written by another great
missionary bearing witness to the cosmic significance
of Jesus Christ, he himself saw a new world and
entered into a new dimension of life. " Jesus Christ
became the centre of everything. . . . From the first
my imagination began to glow with the cosmic significance of Jesus Christ. It was the cosmic Christ
that fascinated me, the living Lord Jesus Christ who
was the centre of a great drama of unity, in which
everything in Heaven and on earth was to become
one in Him. I did not understand what it all meant,
but the tendency to think everything in terms of
Jesus Christ and a longing to contribute to a unity
in Christ became the passion of my life." (Mackay.
Op. cit. Pp. 8-9.)

Through the picture of the incarnate Son of God,

descending, dying, rising, exalted, everything in earth and heaven, the stubborn facts of the thing-world, the complex details of the organic world, and the stern laws of the moral world begin to take on meaning within the embrace of the one comprehensive whole. Once the communicator has caught a glimpse of this vision, neither the myth of his own scientific environment nor the myths of the non-scientific environments of earlier civilisations will seem adequate to interpret the wholeness of reality. In the light of the face of Jesus Christ the imperfection of all impersonal and sub-personal mythologies is revealed. Yet, whenever and wherever that imperfection is recognised and humbly confessed, there is new beginning and new expansiveness. From the new centre of unity, thought and imagination can stretch out to embrace all things, gathering them into their true meaning and final integration in the eternal and transcendent Christ.[1]

[1] For examples of brilliant attempts to work out comprehensive interpretations of the universe in the light of the Christ-revelation, I should turn to Father Lionel Thornton's exposition of the Divine organism in Christ and of recapitulation in Christ or to Paul Tillich's system centring in the New Being in Christ. See L. S. Thornton. *The Incarnate Lord. Revelation and the Modern World.* Paul Tillich. *Systematic Theology.* Vol. I. At the same time, the Rev Colin Elliott has pointed out to me that Martin Johnson in his books on the modern scientific world-view regards models taken from the realms of physics or biology as of merely temporary usefulness and in the long run as inapplicable outside their own quantitative context. See *Science and the Meanings of Truth, Time and the Nebulae.*

CHAPTER EIGHT

The Effective Technique

I. NEW MEANS OF COMMUNICATION

SCIENTISTS ASSURE us that the second Industrial
Revolution has begun. The first was brought about
by the expanding use of the machine and the multi-
plication of manufactured goods. Man dedicated his
labour to the service of the machine and in return
gained possession of increasing numbers of mechanical
appliances and manufactured articles. He did not
cease to be dependent upon the land and the products
of the land ; he was not unmindful of the need for
improved communications in order that his goods
might be advertised and distributed ; but the whole
drive of his energies was set in the direction of
making more efficient machinery and of producing
larger quantities of goods.

The twentieth century, however, has witnessed a
startling change of emphasis. When the history of
this century comes to be viewed in proper perspective
it will probably be judged that the most powerful
instruments of change in human affairs during this
period have been the aeroplane and the radio. Each
is essentially an instrument of communication. By

means of the aeroplane man can span the continents in hours rather than days or weeks ; by means of the radio his voice can be heard around the globe with no delay in transmission. But these two instruments, though at present the most obvious and most dramatic in their effects, do not stand alone. On every side men are bending their energies in the direction of improving still further the means of communication and of conveying " information " in more efficient and economical ways.

Though it is comparatively easy for the layman to take advantage of the amazing facilities now offered to him by the telephone, the cinema, the radio and television, it is more difficult for him to grasp what is happening in the wider world of communication theory and practice. He may read about electronic brains and automatic factories and guided missiles, but these may seem at first sight to be only new examples of the inventive genius of the scientific age. They are new inventions, it is true, but they are more than this. They are expressions of the new direction of technology towards efficiency of communication rather than towards efficiency of production. They are the heralds of the second Industrial Revolution which may change the habits and outlook of men in this age as profoundly as the first affected them in the eighteenth and nineteenth centuries. To quote one assessment of the new situation : " Practically everything depends to some extent upon the efficiency of communications, for information passes along all such systems, electrical, mechanical or human : it flows through the nervous system of the animal body, and in the body social is the vital basis for all activity . . . man's advancement and the progress of civilisations have depended on his ability to receive, to communicate and to record his knowledge. With the ever-increasing flow of information, to-day's claim on these facilities—applied to a still wider field —is greater than ever before, and efforts to improve and extend them are the goals of scientists and inventors in this country and elsewhere." (*The Times*, December 8, 1954.)

It has often been pointed out that the spread of early Christianity was due in no small measure to the network of road-communications which had been magnificently engineered by the Roman technicians and to the existence of the Greek *Koine*, which provided a means of reaching the minds and imaginations of the common people. Nothing can be of greater concern to the Christian evangelist to-day, therefore, than to determine what are the most significant instruments for conveying information to our modern world and what are the language-forms which have the widest currency in ordinary speech.

The question of the transmission of purely technical information need not here concern us. The great new fact of our time in the field of general communication is undoubtedly the growing influence and importance of television. Writing in the B.B.C. Quarterly, Dr. B. Ifor Evans, distinguished man of letters and Provost of University College, London, comments : " Television itself is still in its very infancy. Within ten years, given normal possibilities of development, it will be the major instrument in our cultural life. . . . Television is so brilliant a medium that it must occupy increasingly the leisure of those to whom it is available." In similar vein a noted public figure in England has described television as " probably the most important influence on the human mind since the invention of printing." Already there are signs of revolutionary changes in the techniques of political electioneering and debating as this medium is brought into use, and the worlds of education and commerce are being increasingly affected by it. Quite certainly the Christian Churches cannot afford to neglect the challenge and the potentialities of this most powerful means of communication.

But what is essentially *new* about television? Many of its properties are possessed by the radio, many by the cinema film. But the radio can only make its appeal to the ear, and in spite of the fact that in a limited number of cases communication may be made most effectively without reference to or dependence upon the eye, in general, as Ifor Evans remarks, " the eye and the ear together are irresistible." Again, while it is true that the movie film can appeal both to eye and ear, it suffers from two limitations. It is normally shown in places of public assembly and does not make its impact upon the family unit in its own home. (There are indeed certain group effects produced in a cinema which could not easily be paralleled elsewhere.) Secondly, it cannot reproduce pictures of the living present : that which is shown on the film deals either with the past or with the world of the imagination. Thus television covers a wider range of human experience and appeals to a wider range of human sensitivities in the ordinary settings of life than does any other medium of communication at present in use. It could perhaps be urged that a skilful public speaker or a clever actor would appeal to a wider range of human emotions than is possible for the man who appears on television : at the same time the continuity and the variety and the outreach afforded by television are such as no single speaker or actor could possibly command by the use of individual resources alone.

II. THE IMAGE AND THE WORD IN HISTORY

How then do these new developments affect the communication of the Christian Gospel ? In the course of our inquiry a major division has appeared. On the one side we have come to see the importance of the Image and the Picture and the Myth : through a controlling image all things in heaven and earth are *seen* in proper perspective. On the other side we have recognised the importance of the Word and the Story and the History : through the witness to a determinative cluster of events the history of mankind can be evaluated and interpreted. If, now, we are justified in assuming that the Image and the Word are necessary in every age and in every situation for a full communication of Christian truth, we can begin to see the way in which different techniques of communication have been and can be used to this end.

Let us first take the Image. There must be the continuing disclosure of the Person of the Son before the *eyes* of men. They must be enabled to *see*. It is true that there is a form of inward vision which may not seem to be immediately dependent upon perception : it is also true that words can bring vivid pictures to the human imagination. Yet these two forms of seeing can never make the primary form of direct vision unnecessary or redundant. At every period of Christian history, if communication is to be effective, there must be certain great objectivities related to the Person of the Son of God which people can literally *see*. It need hardly be said that nothing can more effectively disclose Divine sonship than the individual or the community whose pattern of life bears upon it the stamp of the sacrificial career of the Son of God. A Stephen, a church such as that of Corinth, which could be described as a " living epistle," brings vividly before men's eyes the pattern of the sonship to which all have been called and to which, by God's grace, all may be conformed.

But man does not only live in the immediacy of the present. By the images which he constructs he constantly seeks to universalise the vision which he has seen. So through painting and symbolic designs, through sculpture and through architecture, through ritual forms and the mystery-drama, he seeks to placard openly before his own eyes and the eyes of his contemporaries the objectivities and stabilities and regularities of the Divine order which has been revealed to him. For example, the paintings in the Roman catacombs declare the theme of " the wondrous intervention of God in human affairs, for the subjects which occur with almost tedious iteration are those which most clearly proclaim the power of God to intervene in the course of history and against all the odds to deliver the people that put their trust in Him."[1]   Noah, Abraham, Daniel and the three children are depicted again and again as objects of the Divine deliverance. In the case of Christ Himself the favourite image is that of the Good Shepherd for in that picture men saw a salvation which could touch every part of their lives and could bring them safely through the jaws of death into the eternal Kingdom.

Later (from the fifth century onwards) the crucifixion itself became the subject of Christian art, and in the picture of the Son of God reigning from the tree a marvellous image was provided for a comprehensive interpretation of a universe in which disintegration and death were the chief enemies. With the coming of the great age of Gothic architecture it was the turn of buildings to provide the integrating Christian image while in the fifteenth century the mystery-play brought vividly before men's eyes the central myth of their redemption. " I should find it difficult to believe," writes Emïle Mâle, " that anyone listened with much attention to the metaphysical discourses of Justice and Mercy or to the long sermon preached by John the Baptist. But to see Jesus in

[1] R. L. P. Milburn. *Early Christian Interpretations of History*, 97-98.

person, to see Him live and die and rise from the dead before their very eyes—that was what moved the crowd even to tears."[1]   And all the time, through the regular sacramental ministrations of the Church, both in East and West, the Son of God in His cleansing, pardoning, life-sustaining, life-renewing activities was constantly being set forth before the eyes and imaginations of men.   Whatever defects there were in the Christendom of the millenium between A.D. 500 and A.D. 1500 it succeeded to a notable degree in providing visual forms whereby the figure of the Son of God in His descent to earth, His incarnate life, His passion, death and exaltation, came to occupy the central place in the imagination of the age and to be the integrating agent through whom all life was interpreted and controlled.

What the Middle Ages so gravely lacked was any sense of history and of God's purpose being worked out through His servants in history.   And this lack was not unrelated to the neglect of the other supreme means of communication—the Word.   For in every age there must be the proclamation that the central event of history, to which all other histories are related, has happened through the Christ.   Men must *hear* the good news.   There is, it is true, a form of inward-hearing which may not seem to be immediately dependent upon physical sounds : it is also true that the printed page can transmute itself into words that are virtually audible as it makes its impact upon the

[1] Religious Art, p. 111. For the remarkable influence of mural paintings in the churches of fourteenth-century England, see W. A. Pantin. *The English Church in the XIV Century*, 239 ff.

perceptive organs. Yet the oral communication has been the most direct and on the whole the most effective means of proclaiming openly that through the Christ the whole course of human history and the whole character of human destiny have been changed. Again, I need hardly say that nothing more impressively declares this change than the living witness to an actual re-direction from sin to holiness, from self to God, such as have been given by a Saul of Tarsus or a Church of Thessalonica. When men proclaim that as a result of the work of Christ they have themselves turned from idols to serve a living and true God, others begin to recognise the unparalleled proportions of the initiating event.

But there are symbolic expansions of the word as well as of the image. Through varying *forms* of speech —the story and the sermon, the parable and the allegory, the catechetical instruction and the hymn— the Christian evangelist has sought in different ages to proclaim the good news of the great event to his contemporaries. Each of these forms has its own conventions and technical accompaniments which cannot be neglected or ignored. Moreover, some are more suited than others to the purpose of testifying to saving events in history. The instruction and the allegory lend themselves to the presentation of abiding moral principles, the lecture and the credal statement to the confession of unchanging divine truths. Perhaps the parable and the story are the most adequate media for proclaiming the good news of the redemption achieved by Christ. The parable shows *how* the great event breaks into history, the story proclaims that the event *has* broken into history. Each must be related to the patterns of thought and activity current in the first century A.D. ; each must be related to the patterns of the contemporary age.

With all the concentration of interest of the Middle Ages upon the picture of the Christ as Head of a Christian civilisation which seemed so firmly established, there was an almost complete lack of awareness in ecclesiastical circles of the new forces which were working in human history and of the new hopes of national destiny which were taking shape in men's minds. The Reformers saw their own history in the light of New Testament history and vice versa, and when, therefore, they declared in contemporary terms the good news of the deliverance wrought by God in Christ, men listened and were stirred and rose up to take action in the conviction that God was ready to do for them and through them mighty acts after the pattern of the once-for-all historical redemption.

What the Reformed Churches have lacked so gravely has been any kind of comprehensive world-view flexible enough to take in new discoveries and new knowledge. In the main they have neglected visual means of communication, especially when the opportunity arose in the eighteenth century for adventures in evangelism outside the European or new-European environment. Unlike Catholic missionaries who sought to present the central image of their faith and to relate it to the whole symbolic and mythical complex of the culture to which they came,

Protestant missionaries relied almost entirely upon the word and its symbolic expansions. This would not have been so serious if they had been addressing themselves to peoples possessing an awakening sense of historic development and destiny. But in the main this was not the case for throughout the nineteenth century there was little evidence of historical movement amongst the peoples of Africa and the East. It is true that many a missionary through a life of self-giving and compassion reflected a vivid image of the Son of God into the new environment. But in itself this was not enough to re-form a whole culture into the pattern of the Divine image revealed in Christ. The communication needed to make its impact upon both ear and eye if a wholeness of Christian experience was to be created within these new lands.

III. THE POWER OF DRAMATIC FORMS

So far I have virtually separated seeing from hearing in order that the particular relatedness of each might appear more clearly. What can be said finally, however, about the media and techniques of communication which work through eye *and* ear, through the image *and* the word? There is little doubt that the central form by which such a communication can be made is the *drama*. In the drama, words and gestures, ideas and actions, are combined within one comprehensive form which makes its appeal to ear and eye. Moreover, there is the combination of the setting of the drama, which represents a certain stability of structure, with the plot, which is concerned with historical change. From the beginning of Christian history the sacraments have constituted the central dramas. Whenever they have been enacted men have been given an image through which to view reality and a word by which to interpret their historical existence. Often one part of the dramatic complex has been exaggerated at the expense of the other, and then the effectiveness of this particular medium has suffered proportionately. And the same is true of other forms besides the sacraments in which, during the course of Christian history, words and images have been combined for the purpose of proclaiming the Gospel. Religious plays, dramatic sermons, pageants and processions all need to keep the proper balance of sight and sound if they are to represent the wholeness of Christian truth.

In a measure the invention of printing provided a means of appealing to both ear and eye on a scale that had never been possible before. Through this marvellous medium it became possible for men not only to hear the word but to see it, to retain it for further consideration, to interpret it by seeing it within its context. It is true that at first sight they may seem to have *seen* little more than a collection of abstract symbols. But in the case of the Bible in particular (and in a measure this is also true of the great myths and epics and legends of antiquity which were becoming available) the language so often corresponded directly with scenes and places and incidents and so often drew vivid pen-portraits of persons that through reading the Bible men found themselves looking out upon the hills of Palestine and even catching glimpses of the Son of God journeying from Galilee to Jerusalem.

Since the invention of printing other devices have facilitated the extension of the word, while the increasing skill of the photographer has made for the rapid reproduction and distribution of the image. But now at length the medium has been discovered by which word and image together can be instantaneously conveyed and reproduced within wider and wider circles of human life. Much has still to be done to improve transmission and to perfect reception, but there is little doubt that ultimately it will be possible for a person in one part of the world to receive both a visual impression and a verbal message from almost any other part of the world. Surely no medium ever yet discovered offers greater possibilities to the Christian evangelist as he seeks to extend the communication of the Image of God in Christ and of the Good News of what God has done in Christ.

Not that this new medium puts all other means of communication out of court. The importance of the person to person encounter and of the communication through the sacramental drama in a familiar setting cannot possibly be exaggerated. Here are the indispensable media for final and decisive Christian communication. Yet there are these other means, at a lower level of intensity, at a wider range of outreach, but all in some way preparing the ground for the kind of final communication which touches a man at the very depths and limits of his existence. These other means capture the interest, stimulate the imagination, open doors to adventure, offer a way of richer experience. And of these none is so powerful as that which can convey *the symbolic drama and the segment of living experience* into the very homes of the people.

The " symbolic drama " includes actual dramas designed to reinterpret the great characters or the great issues of Biblical history and Church history : dramas designed to interpret contemporary problems in the light of the Christian revelation : cartoons designed to show by the methods of condensation and allusion how the Kingdom of God touches the customs and structures of modern social life. The " segment of living experience " includes examples of Christianity in action in our contemporary world : the work of a mission hospital : the patient labours of a Christian teacher : the adventures of a missionary pioneer : the faithful service of a pastor who is the guide and friend of his people. The cartoon and the Live Action piece have proved to be immensely powerful instruments in the secular use of television and there is no reason why these modern forms, parallel in their way to the parables and the mighty acts which the Gospel story records, should not be employed within the contemporary scene.

Experiments are waiting to be made, techniques are waiting to be investigated. It is perhaps questionable whether television is the best means for communicating certain large aspects of Christian truth and certain critical proclamations of the Christian gospel. At the same time the Christian Churches dare not let this new and most powerful medium go by default. This is not primarily a time for new buildings : nor is it a time for the creation of new institutional machinery. It is a time rather for ensuring that as " information " of all kinds courses through the world's channels of communication the most important " information " ever given to man shall not be left out. For it is certain that the Christian Church cannot afford to neglect any of the established means of communication in any age. Some of the media of mass-communication may be incapable of conveying the abiding and comprehensive proclamations of the Christian Gospel : some may be outside the range of the resources of the Christian Church. But if God's communication to eye and ear is to be effectively transmitted into our modern world, the newspaper and the film, the broadcast and the telecast, must in some way be utilised or the greater part of the world will continue to be unaware that such a communication has ever been made.[1]

---

[1] No longer is it possible for the Christian Church to place an almost exclusive reliance upon the techniques of printing and book-construction and literature-distribution (as through the great Bible societies). Such a warning as is given by Sir B. Ifor Evans in his book, *Literature and Science*, needs to be taken very seriously. " The sovereign place of the printed word," he writes, " is now challenged more vigorously than at any time since the discovery of printing by new and technically agile instruments of distribution capable of addressing audiences of almost illimitable size. We have returned through radio to a new age of oral communication and with the brilliant but dread aid of television we are about to come upon a period when radio may go to the lumber room and a new method of combined oral and visual communication will dominate the scene." And again : " The age of the printed book, which has governed literature and learning since the Renaissance, may be drawing to its close. The mass audience in the technological age will look and listen, with a reception that is controlled, and may largely replace the audience of the printed word, which could exercise its own choice, and indulge in reflection, and repetition." (Pages 7-8).

CHAPTER NINE

The Task of Translation

I. THE RESIDENCE-REQUIREMENT

WE COME finally to the communicator's task of expressing the Christian message in the language of a culture other than his own. As I have already suggested, few tasks in the world are more difficult. A man has grown up within the living organism of his own language : he has become incorporated into it and it has become a part of his own person. But now he is summoned to reverse the process, to return to first principles, to withdraw from the language-world in which he has been living and to enter as a child into another language-organism within which he can begin to grow again. The fact, however, that he is already well advanced within his own language means that he is constantly tempted to adjust himself to the new medium simply by the method of establishing equivalences. Up to a point such a method is legitimate though it can never extend beyond the very limited number of objects or patterns of experience which are virtually the same in every environment. The fundamental truth is that there are only two ways of becoming really incorporated

into a new language medium : one is by living in
the environment where the language has been spoken
for a very considerable period of time ; the other is
by engaging in conversations of all kinds with those
for whom the particular language is the mother-
tongue.

Let us look first at the residence-requirement. It is
a well-known fact that a child born in a particular
country and living in it for a period of three or four
years and then going away, has an enormous advantage
over all others if the time ever comes for him to return
to the country of his birth and to learn its language
afresh. In the early impressionable years the child has
imbibed sound-rhythms and image-patterns which
provide an invaluable preparation for growth in the
language later on. But when there has been no
former contact with the environment of the language
there must be the readiness to go and live within it
—and not within an artificial colony of some foreign
culture established in the land. We are told to-day
that the minimum period for such an acclimatisation
is two years, but for many people it will be far longer.
One man differs from another in sensitivity of eye
and ear and no real growth in the language is possible
until the sound-rhythms and the image-structures
begin to form themselves within the learner's inner
consciousness.

In particular, the importance of learning to *see*
within the new environment has not always been
given proper emphasis. To a very large extent the
citizen of the Western world has grown to maturity

within an environment whose dominant features are stereotyped patterns and abstract symbols. This is certainly true of the town-dweller and it has become increasingly true of those who live in rural communities. Row upon row of houses roughly similar in shape, streets crossing one another in regular straight lines, smoothness and flatness everywhere, uniformity of motion, regularities of light and shade—these are the patterns which the Westerner learns to expect : these have tended more and more to form the framework from within which the rest of reality is seen. Besides these patterns there are the abstract symbols with which the Western child becomes familiar from earliest years. His vision is focused upon shapes, patterns, letters, figures, and by means of generic words—cat, dog, tree, pen—he is encouraged to form general concepts rather than to direct his attention to the concrete image or to the particular object. The result of all this is that the image-language of the modern Western world is formal, abstract and regular. We find it increasingly hard to *see* in any other way. (Though as I pointed out at an earlier stage the images of the unconscious may still have a large part to play in our manner of seeing.)

In the Eastern world and amongst those cultures which have not yet been seriously affected by contacts with Western civilisation, the outlook is very different. Here the dominant features are particular images and concrete symbols. Within a strictly limited environment every variation is noted and conceptualised. The properties of every different kind of tree, the behaviour of every different kind of animal, the way in which an action is performed under every different kind of condition, the particular characteristics of every different kind of human being—all of these are carefully observed : to construct general images or to conceptualise regular forms is exceedingly difficult for one who has grown to maturity in this way. In addition there are exceedingly few abstract symbols. It is true that there are interesting examples of such shapes as the cross and the mandala and the leaf-form to be found amongst divers peoples, but in general whatever symbolism there is tends to be rich in variety, portraying concrete faces, figures, expressions, movements, such as have been observed within the boundaries of the familiar environment. Thus the image-language of the cultural areas which have been relatively stable and self-contained has been picturesque, concrete and rich in variety. To *see* in this way is the normal quality of one who has lived and grown within these surroundings.

For the communicator going from one cultural environment into another the first essential is probably the capacity to *recognise* that this difference of outlook exists. To expect members of a non-Western culture to see at once in terms of his own formal patterns and abstract symbols is obviously to expect the impossible. Rather must he seek to see through their eyes and to become familiar with their general environment. He will pay special attention to their symbolic forms—buildings, carvings, rough sketches, use of colours, decorations. He will watch for variations in the natural order, he will take special note of any records of dreams. In particular he will seek to become acquainted with the people's mythology for in that, as we have seen, the attempt is made to build up a total world-picture through images and sounds. In this way he may hope gradually—though all too gradually it will seem—to see things from their angle and so to be in a position to transpose the central Image of his own faith into the heart of the new cultural environment.

II.   THE CONVERSATION-REQUIREMENT

Let us look now at the second requirement. What I have said of the *visual* environment of the urban communities of the West is in large measure also true of the *verbal* environment, though the fact that men continue to talk to one another about personal matters even in the midst of the most technological of environments means that the process of abstraction and formalisation has not reached such lengths in language as in imagery. Yet the language of the West has become increasingly technical and abstract : it has to be geared to the precise function that is being performed ; it has to be encoded in the most economical way ; it has to deal with the regularities and recurrences which are the characteristic features of factory and generator and atomic pile. But it has also to be related to the increasing organisation of social life. The mass society is workable only when it is operated in largely mechanical ways. So the language necessary for its smooth running takes on mechanical features and the prospect of translating by the aid of the automatic machine comes definitely into view.

Again how different this is from the language, shall we say, of the Arabs. Here *general* terms are at a discount. Names for the camel in every conceivable condition and movement are available ; descriptions of processes in every kind of variation may also be found. Words describing personal characteristics, words required in personal relationships—these are part of the language. The word denotes an imaginable object or action : it does not stand for classes, objects, or for general processes. Obviously this is not entirely the case for if a new word were required to describe every new event a language would soon get entirely out of hand. But amongst dynamic peoples such as the Semites and the Arabs the all-important function of language is to name particular activities or events and to provide a means whereby the members of the tribe can share with one another both the heritage of past history and the realities of present experience.

In spite of the increasingly technical character of the language systems of Western man, he is still very much aware of his history and still very much concerned to live with his fellows (though these characteristics may be growing less pronounced through the very pressure of technological developments). This means that he still has much in common with other tribes and nations who possess some sense of history and of a communal purpose and destiny. The case is, however, more difficult where no such

sense of social history exists. The communicator has
then to be largely content with living, as I have
already suggested, in the *visual* environment. He must
become familiar with the language-forms which
correspond to the images of the natural environment
and to the various functions of the social environment. Where, however, there is a language which is
related to historical event and social encounter the
communicator will seek in every way possible to
catch the attitude to past, present and future which
it reveals and to learn the dynamic of inter-personal
relationships which it contains. He will pay special
attention to the language of ceremonies for these are
of immense importance in social contacts. He will
listen to the legends and songs relating to the past
and will watch for any indications of the hopes of the
future. Above all he will listen to conversations of
every kind and will join in them himself as soon as
he has gained the initial equipment. For a long time
his own inheritance of scientific and abstract terms
will be of little use. But for the *Christian* communicator that is not a matter of special concern seeing
that his message is centred in a personal history and
not in a scientific or an organisational achievement.

Whatever the character of a people's culture and
whatever the stage of its development, the communicator is bound to seek in every way possible to
listen and to speak, to read the literature which
people are reading (if there be vernacular literature)
and to write in the language himself. What W. J.
Bradnock says of the preparation of the translator

can equally well be said of every communicator in whatever new environment he is seeking to make his message known :

" It requires a mental alertness and sensitiveness that misses nothing in the life and culture of the people he would serve. It demands the closest possible identification with every type of person, Christian and non-Christian. He learns his lessons on the roof-top in the morning, in the busy streets in the middle of the day, and by the well in the cool of the evening. He talks ploughs and oxen, seeds and crops with the farmer, listens to the domestic problems of the troubled housewife, tries to follow both sides in disputes of the law court, learns to make jokes with the schoolboy and to make himself rich with the proverbial wisdom of the village headman. If he is very wise he spends long evenings in the dusty villages, listening patiently to the ceaseless conversation of the old men. He will hear tales and folklore that derive from a hoary past and in the process may recognise that he is having his first practical lessons in comparative religion. If he is lucky enough to be invited to weddings or birthday ceremonies or any other festive occasion, he will be grateful for an opportunity *par excellence* of gaining new insights into the life of the people." (*New Light from New Translations*, p. 12.)

III. THE DIFFICULTIES OF COMMUNICATION

All this may seem to be Utopian, a mere counsel of perfection. Who can begin to measure up to such a standard ? In reply I would suggest two things. First that there will ever be men of genius who with sensitivities of vision and hearing which others do not possess will be able to enter into an alien environment and transpose into its language-forms messages of abiding significance. Their work may need to be reviewed and revised from time to time, but their achievements will stand as landmarks in the history of human communication. The task of succeeding translators will be immeasurably lighter because of what they have done. In the second place it is the fact that the communicator to-day has all kinds of aids at his disposal which were not available in former times. Dictionaries, grammars, films, tapes, the researches of anthropologists and historians, the beginnings of native art, literature in the vernacular —all help to smooth the way for the evangelist seeking to express his message in language-forms which are authentic and meaningful. In the main, communication is no longer a task with which the individual has to wrestle in isolation. Other men have laboured and are labouring and he can enter into their labours.

Yet it is still true that any form of transposition continues to be an immensely difficult task. It is so easy to miss the proper wavelength. On the one side there has to be the continual struggle to get to the very heart of the truth which is to be communicated. " The art of transposing truths," wrote Simone Weil, " is one of the most essential and the least known. What makes it difficult is that, in order to practise it, one has to have placed oneself at the centre of a truth and possessed it in all its nakedness, behind the particular form in which it happens to have found expression." (*The Need for Roots*. 65.) On the other side there has to be the continual effort to pierce to the very heart of the environment into which the communication is to be made. It may be to the heart of the community : it may be to the heart of the individual. " What is the function of the dramatist ? " asks Gabriel Marcel. " It is certainly not to mount into a pulpit ; indeed each time he tries to preach he betrays his mission. His task is rather to place himself at the very heart of human reality, in all its poignancy and intimacy. He must, it seems to me, link himself magnetically to the strands of our most secret agonies and our most secret hopes ; and the accent with which he expresses feelings we hardly dare admit even to ourselves, must be strong enough and magical enough to transfigure our interior landscape and illuminate it in a flash with a light that seems to come from beyond." (*Three Plays*. 32-3.)

To place oneself at the heart of the truth—this, I have suggested, involves a constant return to the image of the Son of God in His self-emptying and self-fulfilment, a constant response to the good news of the Christ Who lived and died and rose again. This is not the truth in all its nakedness but it is truth whose light can illuminate the whole of reality, it is truth whose pattern can give meaning to the whole of man's historical existence. On the other side, to place oneself at the heart of human reality—this, I have suggested, involves an identification with the neighbour at the point from which he looks out upon the wholeness of his universe, a meeting with the neighbour at the place where he comes to terms with his past and looks forward into his future. Whatever I can learn of the *details* of the Christian world-picture and of the Christian interpretation of history will help me—but the central Image and Word are alone indispensable : whatever I can learn of the *details* of my neighbour's world-picture and of his view of history will be of value—but again the centre of his vision and of his interpretation are alone essential. So to present the Image that the neighbour allows it to become *his* image, so to proclaim the Word that the neighbour welcomes it as *his* word, this is the communicator's task and glory in every age.

IV. THE PARABLE OF THE SOWER

Even when every attempt has been made to ensure that message, messenger, techniques and language-forms are the best possible for the task of communicating the Divine revelation, it still remains true that new difficulties are constantly arising and that ancient systems of thought and action long entrenched do not readily open channels for the entrance of new information. At the same time, if the Christian Doctrine of the Spirit has any validity at all, it means that the Holy Spirit is constantly working in the world to bring about a more effective communication and a more penetrating apprehension of the Image and Word of God : it means, too, that those who are seeking, in all sincerity and with all patience, to engage in the work of communication can be assured of the assistance of the Holy Spirit Whose joy it is to take of the things of Christ and reveal them unto men.

In considering the difficulties of the task it is important to remember that even Jesus Himself was not exempt from the unresponsiveness and the resistance of the world of His day. His first recorded parable makes it clear that there were human " soils " into which the seed of the Divine Word might fall but from which no useful harvest could be expected. In the main the defective soil was either too shallow or too crowded, either open to any and every fleeting impression, unchecked by any kind of critical judgment, or so preoccupied with secular concerns that the things of the spirit had no chance to take root and grow. In the one case every seed of communication just came and went ; there were no deep stirrings or wrestlings of the imagination to which it could appeal. In the other case every seed of communication was strangled at birth : the rank weeds of material acquisitiveness and physical lust were too strong for the newcomer to establish a place in their midst.

This diagnosis of the human condition in relation

to the coming of the Divine Word has lost none of
its penetration as we survey the contemporary world.
It is not a religious leader but a noted literary critic
who has said that we are seeing to-day " the first
society of the Western world not based upon the
religious imagination but based directly and pre-
cariously upon the secular and experimental imagination, so far as it is based at all." (R. P. Blackmur.
Language as Gesture. P. 420.)

I would suggest that the " experimental " corresponds exceedingly closely to the shallow soil of
Jesus' parable, the " secular " to that which was
thorn-infested.   Where there are no roots in the
tradition of a living social organism it is extraordinarily
hard for the individual to exercise a balanced critical
judgment.   When he is surrounded on all sides by
material goods to be acquired and by sensuous
pleasures to be pursued, it is almost impossible for
him to give proper attention to the values of the spirit.
In fact it is not fanciful to see conditions of *soul*
erosion developing in the common humanity of
modern technological man comparable to the tragic
state of *soil* erosion which affects large areas of the
earth's surface to-day.   If human nature begins to
approximate to a dust-bowl condition no amount of
skilful communication can produce moral or spiritual
fruit to perfection.

In the second place, Jesus was well aware that His
" mighty works," however impressive they might be
to those who had eyes to see, failed to elicit any serious
response from many of His contemporaries.   " Woe

unto thee, Chorazin! woe unto thee, Bethsaida! for if the mighty works had been done in Tyre and Sidon, which have been done in you, they had a great while ago repented, sitting in sackcloth and ashes." " If thou hadst known, even thou, at least in this thy day, the things which belong unto thy peace ! but now they are hid from thine eyes." " O ye hypocrites, ye can discern the face of the sky ; but can ye not discern the signs of the times ? " Though events were taking place openly in history, though Jesus Himself was performing actions which men could clearly see, all too often there was either indifference or an irresponsible suggestion that these visible signs were nothing more than evidences that an evil power was active in their midst.

In this respect, perhaps the most sinister development of our own day is the proliferation of the means of communication to the point where ordinary folk are being bombarded, day in and day out, by images and words. Through slogans, through catch-words, through cartoons, through the pictures of commercial art, through propaganda, through news and news-commentaries, through the manifold, devices of radio and television, man's receptive organs are being stimulated, startled and often stunned. After a while his reactions become less marked and the stage may even be reached where he ceases to react altogether. He may simply abandon himself to the control of whatever force seeks to lead him : or he may become numb and impassive, unable to respond to any external stimulus at all.

A great deal of research waits to be done on the whole subject of " communications-fatigue." What produces maximum or minimum response ? When is the limit to effective response reached ? What are the relative values of variation and repetition ? These questions need further investigation, but what is certain is that in a world in which information of every kind is being poured through channels of every kind it is becoming increasingly difficult for the distinctively Christian communication to gain a hearing or to win any response. So many mighty works are being done, so many historical events are being seen, so many processes of the natural order are being unveiled, that Divine works, Divine events, Divine processes seem of little account. Why pay attention to them ? Are they not just as likely to be products of natural selection or of chance forces ? To-day, as in Jesus' day, there is no *guarantee* that the exhibition of or the witness to the mighty works of God will not be either ignored or misunderstood.

Perhaps most serious of all the obstacles to the spread of Christian communications is the resistance of established views of the universe and interpretations of history. In Jesus' day the reign of Law seemed supreme ; the " chosen people " interpretation of history seemed impregnable. How could the new communication break through these impenetrable walls ? And so it is to-day when the mechanistic view of the universe still holds almost unchallenged sway and when history is interpreted in terms either of national Messianism or of political Utopianism. There are, as Paul Tillich has pointed out,[1] situations in which a tradition and a myth, firmly entrenched, can make it almost impossible for a new interpretation to gain a hearing. Certainly to-day it is far from easy for the Christian message to be taken seriously in a world where scientific advances and power politics seem all-important.

Yet the communication must be made. In a striking passage in his book *The Theology of the New Testament* (Vol. I), Rudolf Bultmann remarks : " In the cross of Christ Jewish standards of judgment and human notions of the splendour of the Messiah are shattered. Thus, the acknowledgment of the Crucified as Messiah implicitly contains a new understanding of man-before-God." (46.) This was the situation in the Jewish world of the first century. But equally in reference to the *Greek* world of that day we could write : " In the career of the incarnate Son of God Greek standards of judgment and human notions of the impassibility of the Logos are shattered. Thus the acknowledgment of Jesus as the Logos, the meaning of the whole universe, implicitly contains a new view of human nature in relation to the Divine." There had to be a great breaking down before there could be a building up and all real communication must involve a similar process.

Coming forward to our own day, it is probably unnecessary to pay too much attention to the local myths and limited social histories still firmly held in many parts of the world. As we have seen, the all-

[1] *The Interpretation of History*, p. 55.

important factors in the modern world are the myths associated with the scientific world-view and the interpretation of history expressed either through some form of political idealism, or through some form of communistic materialism. Over against these the Christian Gospel stands. Do we dare to affirm that " In the pattern of sacrifice revealed through the career of the Son of God, all impersonal standards of scientific judgment and human notions of the invincibility of technological man are shattered. Thus the acknowledgment of the Crucified as expressing the ultimate meaning of the universe implicitly contains a new view of the Divine integration of human life " ? Or again is it possible to claim that : " In the cross of Christ all sub-personal standards of historical judgment and human notions of the inevitability of material progress are shattered. Thus the acknowledgment of the Crucified as the Saviour of all history implicitly contains a new understanding of the Divine reconciliation at work in human life " ? Such claims will inevitably provoke resistance, however attractively communicated. There is no expeditious road to pack and label men for God; there is likewise no guaranteed form of effective communication. Always the struggle must continue. The end is never in sight.

V.   IMAGINATIVE IDENTIFICATION AND RECIPROCAL INTERCHANGE

Is it possible to sum up in two final terms the secret of the communication to eye and ear which has been the subject of this book? I believe that it is. The first I take from a broadcast entitled "The Problem of Communication," given by F. A. Cockin, the Bishop of Bristol, early in 1953. The term is *imaginative identification*. The communicator must try, he says, to understand why the other man cannot see or make sense of things which mean much to the committed Christian. "Why is he the kind of person he apparently is? What is his home background? What kind of education has he had, maybe purely technical and scientific? What sort of job is he working in, and what are the influences which that job is exercising on his whole outlook? What sort of deal has life given him? Is it likely that, with his general conditioning, he could very easily believe in God, or that he would want to believe in God, when you think of how little such belief seems to square with the world as he sees it?"

Imaginative identification : it is the way of the artist. He is constantly seeking to identify himself with those for whom he is doing his work. At the same time he is constantly seeking to gain a greater mastery of the material which he has chosen as his medium. The architect tries to live intensely, in the realm of the imagination, the kind of life which each of the human types for whom he is providing is bound to experience. At the same time he seeks to learn the properties and the possibilities of the material with which he must work. Now at length his vision, his vicarious living and his technical virtuosity find their unity in the work of art. Through the medium of that which can be seen and heard the spirit of the creative individual touches the spirit of a wider humanity and the life of the whole society is enriched and blessed. But without the intense imaginative identification the end could never have been achieved.

The second term I define as *reciprocal interchange*. True communication can never be a one-way process. To quote again from Mr. Bradnock's pamphlet : " At an early stage in his experience every missionary worth his salt makes certain significant discoveries. He learns not only that the Christian believer has an inescapable responsibility to give the Word to others, but that he must be prepared to receive new light and insight into its deepest meanings as it takes root in the hearts of his people and flowers forth in new cultural settings." (11.) But it is not only as it takes root in the hearts of the people—it is actually in the excitement of the interchange that new meaning breaks out. Here is one of the greatest of life's mysteries and at the same time one of its greatest wonders. If the attempt be made to " store " and " isolate " information it deteriorates and ultimately petrifies. But in the process of communication the information can be sparked to new life and suffused with the glow of new meaning, always provided that there has been a coming together of mind with mind, word with word, person with person, in a truly reciprocal relationship.

Imaginative identification. Did not God identify Himself in imagination (His Wisdom) with man's needs and did He not fashion a pattern of life (the life of the Son of His Love) which, when expressed in and through humanity, set before the eyes of men an eternal object for contemplation and drew man's inner spirit, as by a magnetic power, to abandon its wanderings and illusions and to become reintegrated into the same Divine pattern?

"The life was made manifest, and we saw it, and testify to it, and proclaim to you the eternal life which was with the Father and was made manifest to us."

Reciprocal interchange. Did not God in His mercy enter into a continuing conversation with mankind? Did He not accept human language-forms and gestures to make His own purpose known? Did He not clothe Himself in saving Names and express Himself in healing Actions, as He related Himself to man's broken situation? And did not men crucify the Name and repudiate the Action? And yet did not the Purpose dance with meaning and did not the sundered relationship leap towards its reconciliation in the very place where man said "No" to God's "Yes," but where God answered "Yes" to man's "No"?

"God was in Christ reconciling the world to Himself. We beseech you, in Christ's name: Be ye reconciled to God."

THE END

Index

INDEX